THE CHANGE CYCLE HANDBOOK

How to initiate, implement,
and institutionalize change

Cover Design:
Bill Lavender
Book Design:
William Lannes

Editorial Assistants:
Erin Gendron

Printed in the USA

ISBN: 0-9728143-9-6
ISBN 13: 978-9728143-9-3

University of New Orleans Publishing
Managing Editor
Bill Lavender

UNO Press
UNO Metro College
New Orleans, LA 70148
http://unopress.uno.edu

THE CHANGE CYCLE HANDBOOK

WILL LANNES

Contents

PREFACE

This Handbook is the result of extensive notes used for a Change Management course at the University of New Orleans in Engineering Management and cross listed with the College of Business. The notes were printed by the UNO printing service as a campus course packet to be used during the course. During the numerous semesters in which the course was offered the notes had two major revisions, each revision added an important new chapter. The last chapter added was on the relationship of Change Management to Six Sigma. All of the revisions are included in this first public printing. In regard to Six Sigma I believe that part of the success that Six Sigma has achieved is because of some built in processes in the Six Sigma approach to improvement which are based on change management principles. I believe it is important that this is recognized because it implies if you want to be successful change management principles should be integrated in all new initiatives. That last revision of the notes also introduced the concept of change management competency which is a necessary ingredient to not only succeed in change projects but in sustaining the change. As emphasized throughout of this Handbook, sustaining the change relates to the important topic of institutionalization which is one of the corner stones of this handbook. Change management competency is becoming a needed skill in all organizations and is an important ingredient in institutionalizing change.

It should be noted that the Handbook contains information and data that were a result of the major changes due to Hurricane Katrina. Hurricane Katrina was the most damaging and costly storm to hit the United States in its history and was a natural laboratory to study change. On August 29, 2005, Katrina slammed into the Gulf Coast of the United States. The storm caused major damage and has changed the Gulf Coast and New Orleans in many ways. The storm did, however, also offer many opportunities to observe and experience major change. Those experiences and lessons learned have been captured in this Handbook, primarily in Chapter 11. Unfortunately, the storm also interrupted some change management research which was underway so in Chapter 9 the Northrop Grumman example ends with Katrina rather than with conclusions on the success of the utilization of the change management tools advocated in this book. However that effort emphasized the need to understand how to guide change in the midst of a major crisis so I have included a whole chapter, Chapter 11, on that topic.

There certainly continues to be a wealth of articles and books on change, change management, and similar topics. This is probably due, in part, to the fact that change is such a constant in our lives. Dealing with change also takes a lot of our energy. Hence, we are frequently looking for ways to manage or control change. Much of the literature addresses these issues. So what can this book add to the literature on change? This book primarily emphasizes what most of the previous literature fails to do, that is, *the importance of a methodology on how to institutionalize change -- how to make change last.* Most change management literature concentrates on the implementation phase of change. By "institutionalize", it is meant that change becomes part of the way business is done from that day forward. In other words, the change becomes part of the culture and therefore, is no longer considered as "change". Rather, it is considered the new status quo. Without the institutionalization of change, the change initiative is short lived and simply becomes one more plan of the month/year. *Without this last step, change does not actually occur.* This is also related to the development of a change management competency in an organization. When organizations develop internal change management competency, it helps to foster a culture of change; both are needed if change is going to be institutionalized. This Handbook also contains chapters on two important topics previously mentioned but not found in most change management books. That is , Chapter 11, Managing Change in the Midst of Crisis and another chapter that recognizes that most successful implementation programs have change management built into their process, such as the example of Six Sigma in Chapter 10, Six Sigma and Change Management.

Change in organizations is never ending, it is a continuous cycle of beginnings and endings. Each change initiative itself goes through a cycle of three phases. What I call the Change Cycle is the normal three steps of initiating, implementing, and institutionalizing change. These three phases have to be considered as a whole when initiating change. In this Handbook we emphasize each phase, with institutionalizing being the most important phase. Institutionalizing change means that the change is no longer a change but has been incorporated into the way we do things. This is the real goal of lasting change.

Who would benefit most from this book? Primarily it is for those in business and industry who are struggling with the myriad of change that they face on almost a daily basis. Those involved in this struggle will become overwhelmed if they do not understand change and know how to deal successfully with it. This book will help. It will not only help you with step by step principles and techniques but it will help you understand the whole concept of change. Armed with this understanding, you will be better able to cope with change. This book can also be used for students of change, as has been demonstrated by its successful use for over five semesters at the University of New Orleans in the Change Management course. The University of New Orleans is one of the few universities offering a course solely on change management. The Change Management course has been very popular and each semester its enrollment must be limited because there are always more students who want to take the course than can be accommodated. It can be used as a primary or supplemental textbook at the graduate and senior undergraduate level.

The three phases of change are related but separate phases, the initiation phase, the implementation phase, and the institutionalization phase. These phases are sequential, with unique requirements. However, each phase has elements which are required to be carried forth to the next phase. The phases will be addressed using principles and techniques which can be applied either to new initiatives or to learn from past initiatives by benchmarking. Benchmarking past initiatives to these principles will help you to determine why past initiatives may have failed and what to avoid or what to improve on future change initiatives. Understanding and applying these principles and techniques will not guarantee success of a proposed change; however, it will allow you to analyze the initiative and determine *why* it did or did not succeed. That experience will pay dividends on future change initiatives. The truth is that while change is complex, the successful initiating, implementing, and institutionalizing of change initiatives does follow certain universal principles and techniques, which can be developed into a reusable template. The template developed in this book is a Worksheet for each phase. This is what you will find in this book.

Validation of the principles presented in this book by benchmarking your own experiences to them is a powerful tool for addressing future change initiatives. This type of benchmarking provides the confidence needed to be successful in future initiatives. This combination of principles with experience is the point W. Edward Deming, the well know quality guru, made many years ago in discussing the theory of knowledge as part of his Profound Knowledge System. Deming emphasized that knowledge is not possible without theory, and experience alone does not establish a theory. Deming went on to say that experience only describes. It cannot be tested or validated, and alone is no help in management. On the other hand, theory shows a cause-and-effect relationship that can be used for prediction[1]. The change cycle Worksheets are developed from sound theory and principles. *Hence, coupled with experience gained by using the Worksheets, it can provide an effective means to predict the probable success of future change initiatives.*

In the development of the applicable principles and techniques I have relied heavily on the previously mentioned change literature and my own experiences. Hence, at the end of each chapter there are notes and references for further reading for those who would like additional depth on the concepts presented in each chapter. In regard to the references, I make particular use of many of the concepts in Daryl Conner's book , *Managing at the Speed of Change*. He has done an excellent job in developing such things as the definition of major change and the roles of different persons in the change process such as sponsors, agents, and targets. My introduction to Daryl Conner came many years ago while I was working in the electric utility industry during an Edison Electric Executive Program in Hershey, Pennsylvania. He conducted a one-day seminar on change management. I was struck by how understandable he made a seemly complex subject and how useable his concepts were. This became a goal of this book, to integrate applicable principles and techniques into a simple template which will significantly improve chances of successful implementation of change. Many of the examples I use in the book come from my own experience. I have found in my teaching career that by using these examples students, particularly those with significant industry backgrounds, are often more willing to relate some of their similar work experiences. This creates an exchange of experiences that often validates the principles and greatly assists the learning and retention process and we all learn more, including the instructor. Some of those examples are in this book and, hopefully, when you come across these examples you will pause and think about how they might relate to your own circumstances. I think you will find this helpful. At the end of each chapter are also some suggested exercises. These exercises are designed to reinforce the principles covered in the chapter and to assist in your understanding of these principles.

Since I have indicated that some of the principles and techniques have come from my own experiences I should at least give a brief overview of those experiences. I am no stranger to change. I have been through three major career changes and within those three careers I have had a diversity of assignments. My first career was as an officer in the United States Marine Corps. I spent eleven years in the Marine Corps and had assignments which ranged from training reserves to combat assignments in Vietnam. I had two very different military specialties, electronics and infantry, resulting in some very different assignments. While serving in Vietnam, I was part of the United States Marine Corps Combined Action Program, a unique pacification effort to win the minds and hearts of the people. My next career stop was the longest, twenty-two years in the electric utility industry. There I was primarily involved in engineering and management. As an engineer I was the primary design engineer for a method of uprating the voltage level of electric substations by using arrestors while leaving the insulation level essentially unchanged. We energized the first uprated substation in the United States. These pioneering efforts were the primary reason I was elected as a Fellow in the Institute for Electric and Electronic Engineers. In my latter years in the electric utility industry I held executive positions of Vice President and Senior Vice President and led several large engineering groups through numerous reorganizations efforts. In that role I worked closely with large consulting firms such as McKinsey and Booz-Allen. This period of intensive change gave me an appreciation of the need for a more organized approach to change.

My next career change was to become a faculty member at the University of New Orleans. I was at UNO from 1992 until 2006, at which time I retired with the title of Professor Emeritus. I presently still support the university on special projects, seminars, and occasional classes; most of them related to change management. Almost immediately upon my arrival at UNO I became involved in leading the effort for initiating, implementing, and institutionalizing a new Master of Science of Engineering Management program. The program was requested by industry in 1993. It officially began in 1996, and to date we have graduated well over a 100 students with masters degrees. The program continued to grow and in 2002 we have added a Ph.D. program. Despite Katrina and the need to downsize the UNO faculty, the program continues today. It was during my teaching, research, and consulting efforts associated with the engineering management program that I came to realize there was a need for this Handbook. In fact, much of the development of this book has come directly from my efforts to introduce new methods developed through university research into industry and to incorporate some of these templates into my courses. My background in industry and teaching has led me to the conclusion that knowledge imparted in classes and books should be both used and useful. This is one of the reasons I used the word 'handbook' in the title, it is designed to be a step by step aid in making change successful. I believe that if you apply this test to the principles and techniques described in this book, you will find that it meets that criteria. I hope you enjoy this book, but most of all I hope you find it useful.

Finally, a word about the organization of the book; the first few chapters of the book deal with some of the fundamental aspects of the subject, such as "What is Change." This is important foundational material for the later chapters and I recommend they be read prior to those chapters which outline the template on how to initiate, implement, and institutionalize change. The Worksheets incorporate many of the principles of change management and also includes some unique techniques such as the Project Organizational Relationship Chart which not only assists in properly identifying the sponsor, agent, and target but is the first step in determining who is involved in the project. The Handbook also uses an adaptation of Fisher and Welsolkowski approach to answering the question of "Who is affected and How?" Understanding the how, will help you to locate and understand the potential resistance to the change .The later chapters deal with applying the template in the form of Worksheets to your own company. The last chapter is devoted to the people who will have to carry out the change, those who will have to change, and those who will sustain the change. No change process will work without competent, motivated people. Once you have read the book, I encourage you to try the template on new projects or benchmark it against an old project and let me know the results. I can be reached through my email address, wlannes@uno.edu. I am very much interested in continuing to learn along with you.

Will Lannes
Professor Emeritus

Spring, 2008

Chapter 1

WHAT IS CHANGE?

"Nothing is permanent but change."
Heraclitus

It might be interesting to ask this question, "What is change?" Change can mean very different things for many of us so you might be surprised as to the variance in the answers. While it is true we could probably provide a fairly correct technical definition such as change is the transition period we go through while moving from one state to a different state, it probably will be of little help in understanding the variance of the answers we receive. This variance is due, in large measure, to the perceptions of change by the individual respondents to the question. It is generally well accepted that "perception is reality." This different perception provides some explanation as to why, when some companies face a challenging changing environment they are overwhelmed and often fail while other companies facing this very same environment not only survive, but excel. Often the difference is whether or not we see change as a positive or a negative, as something normal in the course of business or something that disrupts our status quo; different perspectives of change such as these definitely affect our concept of change.

So if change is more than the definition of the transition period of moving from one state to another, then what is it? Actually it consists of two primary parts: the first is un-emotional which refers to the definition and simply helps us understand that change is a transition. The second part, and probably the most important part, is how we react to that transition. That is usually is very much dependent on the personality of an individual or the culture of an organization experiencing the transition. This reaction is often emotional and is why we often experience so much resistance to change.

How we handle change, that is, how we react to the transition, is very important as to whether or not the transition will be successful. Hence, we must understand both the nature of change as well as how we to react to it before we can begin our discussion of how to initiate, implement, and institutionalize change. That is the purpose of this first chapter. Fortunately, there is a great deal of information about change which will be useful to us in preparing for how to initiate, implement, and institutionalize change. Much of this comes from Daryl Conner, an author and consultant, who deals solely with change and how to understand change. We will use some his concepts, particularly his concepts on the role of individuals in change and his concepts of what constitutes major change to help us understand change. If we can understand change, it will feel natural to us. Hence, our perception of change will be that it is normal and we can handle it. This will greatly enhance our chances of success during the transition.

Major Change

Most would agree that if a change is minor it can easily be absorbed into our existing activities and generally is not disruptive and of little concern. However, if the change is major, we often are overwhelmed. So one of the first things we have to address is what is the difference between minor and major changes?

Since we have stated that perception is reality then it should not be a surprise that an important definition of major change is that any change should be considered major when it is *perceived to be so* by those affected.[1] It is extremely important to understand this. Just because you, as the initiator of a change, think it is minor does not make it minor. This is determined by the people who are affected by the change; if the employees think it is major and it is not treated as major, the organization will probably experience many problems in implementing the change. This brings up an important point. That is, if you can determine that the change is believed to be major due to perceptions based on wrong or poor information, then this presents an opportunity to address the situation and change the perception and reduce resistance to that change. I have actually experienced this while working in industry. Our company often introduced new changes at the executive level and then rolled them out to the rest of the organization. When the executive group was first introduced to a new change initiative, there was often concern and doubts expressed by some of the executives. Usually after months of discussing with consultants and benchmarking against others who had implemented this type of change, we would come to a consensus that the change was actually more aligned with our plans than first realized and we were all eager to initiate the change. We would then roll out the initiative to the next level and, in the beginning, were always surprised at the resistance. However, we soon realized that most of the resistance was due to the same doubts and concerns we had experienced when we were first introduced to the change initiative, but we had failed to provide the information from the consultants and benchmarking along with some time to discuss and absorb the new information. Once we realized this, our change initiatives went much more smoothly. The point is that while perception is reality and we must initially accept that - if the perception is based on poor or wrong information this can, and should, be corrected before the process of initiating, implementing, and institutionalizing begins.

There are some other more direct means of defining major change than just relying on perception. One means is the balance between the organization's capabilities and the challenges the organization faces. Many will often see the new challenges as beyond their capabilities. When there is general agreement that the challenge of the change exceeds the organization's capability this can often be fixed with additional training, improved resources (software, computing capability, etc.), or even the acquisition of the required skills through hiring or consultants. Another definition of major change is when the reality of the change is very different from expectations.[2] This often happens when we promise too much to get approval of a project. For example, it may have been claimed that a new software initiative would only take three months for the conversion to be up and running but as soon as the implementation begins it becomes obvious that it will take at least seven months. Suffice to say that if this is not addressed, the change could overwhelm the organization and cause the implementation to fail. Hence, it is important when initiating change to ask if the organization has the capabilities to successfully implement the change and if the reality of the change will closely match the expectations communicated. Perhaps it is because of my engineering background but I like to think of these two questions as two equations that need to be in balance if we are going to succeed. That is, if the challenge is greater than the capabilities or if the reality is worst than the expectations, then they need to be put into balance by adjusting milestones, adding resources or by other means. Without being in balance, the change may fail. The final, and perhaps the best, definition of major change is that change is major when the change is very different from the existing way of doing things (the culture). Note that this definition of major change does not have anything to do with the complexity or cost of the change. The only point is how different the change is from the existing culture.

Positive and Negative Change

It is probably true that most of us think of change as negative. This may be due to the fact that change generally takes us out of our comfort zone of the status quo. However it is important to note that the nature of change is the same whether the change is positive or negative. That is important because if we do not do the same degree of planning and preparation for positive change as we would for negative change, we jeopardize the success of the implementation. This should be kept in mind when organizations approach changes which are universally accepted as positive. Again, the key question is not whether the change is positive or negative, but rather whether it is major or minor. Some examples of positive changes which can be considered major changes for individuals are promotions, relocations, and marriage. It should be noted that the principles and techniques developed to ensure the successful initiation, implementation, and institutionalization of change applies as well to individuals as it does to organizations. Perhaps if we spent more time on properly addressing the steps of initiating, implementing, and institutionalizing marriage, there would be less divorce.[3]

Culture and Its Effect on Change

It is my belief that the most important factor affecting change in an organization is the organization's culture, which is similar to the personality of an individual. Perhaps the best way to describe the culture of an organization is that culture represents "the way we do things." It is what an organization believes and how it acts. You can usually deduce the culture of an organization from the stories it tells. Company stories are a verbal history which emphasize values and beliefs through stories about its heroes, past and present. These heroes are not necessarily the key managers or executives. They are often those company persons whose actions are most memorable and whose actions are generally used when asked to describe the company culture and its values.

Culture serves a very important function by protecting the status quo, but this is where it comes into direct conflict with change. If a proposed change is not aligned with the culture of the organization, it will eventually fail. It will simply become another "program of the month." It will become the type of change in which people in the organization ask, "Whatever happened to that initiative we had a couple of years ago. It seems so promising?" These projects or initiatives will see some initial success and adoption, but they will not be sustained and the organization will not even know why they disappeared. The reason is that the change was not aligned with the culture and when that happens *the culture always wins!*

In his seminars, Daryl Conner uses an arrow diagram, which unfortunately does not appear in his book. I think the diagram is extremely useful in making the point about the importance of culture and its effect on change. He uses the diagram to make a visual point on what is major change. He calls the primary arrow in the diagram the Established Expectation Patterns, which is again another way of saying the culture of the organization. I have used a modified diagram to show the importance of the alignment of culture and the proposed changes. The modified diagram is shown in Figure 1.1.[4]

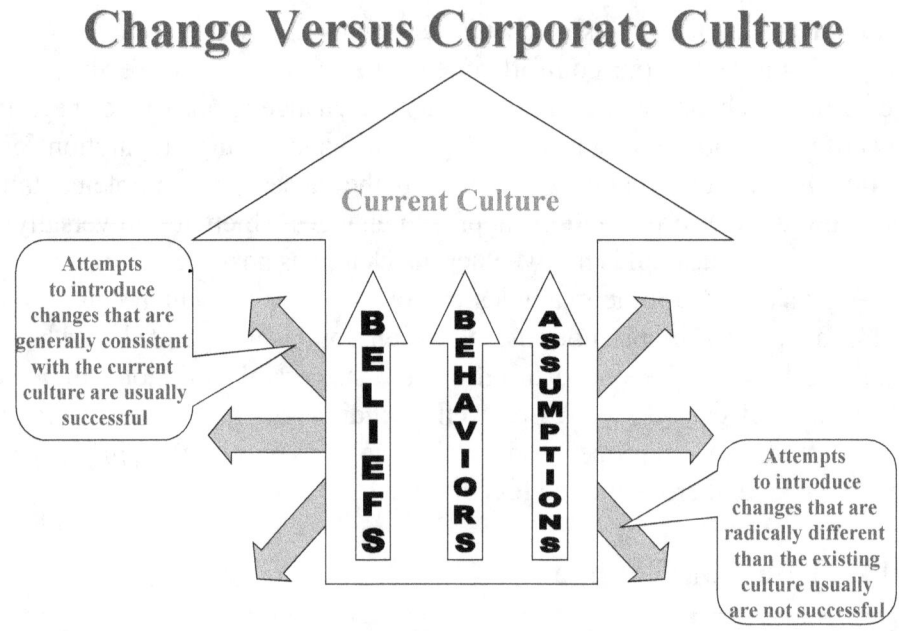

Figure 1.1 Alignment of Corporate Culture and Change

This diagram can constantly remind the reader of the need for alignment of the existing culture with the proposed change. If the proposed change is nearly aligned with the existing culture (or at least in the same general direction), the change will probably be absorbed by the culture and become institutionalized. If there is very poor alignment, or worst if the change is in opposition to the culture, the change will become another "program of the month." More about this will be said later in Chapter 7.

Roles of People in the Change Process

Hopefully by the time you finish this book you will realize that one of my strong beliefs is the importance of trusting the people in your organization. This belief probably had its origin in my first career in the United States Marine Corps. The Marines are strong believers in teamwork and in the expectation that each member of the team will do his duty. This is exemplified in the well known Marine Esprit de Corps as well as in the motto "Semper Fidelis", or "always faithful". To be more to the point, any successful change in an organization can usually be traced to the individual and to team efforts of the people in the organization. Thus, it is important that we look at the roles of people in the change process. Again, I will refer to the definitions as provided by Conner.[5] There are three primary roles people play in the change process. A fourth role is mentioned which is similar to one of the three roles, however with a significant difference. The roles as defined as:

Sponsor: Individual or group who has the power to sanction or *legitimize the change.*

Agent: Individual or group who is *responsible for actually making the change.*

Target: Individual or group who *must actually change* — is the target.

Advocate: Individual or group who wants to achieve the change but lacks the power to legitimize.

The first three categories are fairly common descriptions; however, it is also usual for others to describe the "target" as the "adopter." Adopter is probably a more appropriate name and throughout this book either term will mean the same thing.[6] What is important about this list are the definitions of Sponsor and Advocate. The distinction between the two may seem subtle, but will turn out to be very significant. The distinction is, of course, that one can legitimize the change and the other cannot. Perhaps an example of this difference will help. Suppose that there is in a group or department an outstanding IT professional who constantly keeps up with new software developments and is the in-house expert on software systems, applications, and problem solving. If he or she advocates the use of a new software package for use in the office, based on his/her expertise and knowledge, there will be many who will follow the lead and advocate the adoption of the software. And, in fact, the software may be purchased and with the support of this IT professional, be applied. However, since the adoption was based on expertise rather than the power to legitimize the adoption, it is likely that in the first crisis to follow, whether it be re-organization, budget cuts, or some other major disruption, the software will not be supported and dropped from use. On the other hand, if the expert sought and received sponsorship from the person who could legitimize the change, it will in all likelihood survive the crisis. This is important to remember since many of us have heard that to be successful with change you need a "champion" for the change. Unfortunately, most never seem to differentiate between whether the "champion" is a Sponsor or an Advocate. Without sponsorship, the change will never be institutionalized and will become just another "program of the month."

Innovation and Change

Innovation, invention, or idea generation all represent activities which lead to change. In fact, some would say change can not (or should not) occur without one of these related activities. New product or process development includes both idea generation or invention and innovation. R. Ray Gehani, in his book, *Management of Technology and Operations,* describes the new product development in seven stages, as indicated below.[7]

> Stage 1. Generation of new ideas
> Stage 2. Screening of Generated Ideas
> Stage 3. Technological Feasibility Analysis
> Stage 4. Business Feasibility Analysis
> Stage 5. New Product Testing and Evaluation
> Stage 6. Pilot Testing and Evaluation
> Stage 7. Scaling-up and Commercialization

Similar steps can be found in other product and process development literature. However, some say that the stages can be reduced into two steps – invention and innovation, because some consider innovation the action of putting into use a new idea or invention. Arno Penzias, a venture partner in New Enterprise Associates, states, "You have to start with invention. It's the creative product of the human mind. But innovation means changing somebody's world."[8] If you accept this approach then the change cycle: initiating, implementing, and institutionalizing change could just as correctly be called the innovation cycle. Indeed, the change cycle should be considered as action oriented. We must do something if we want change to happen.

In this chapter we have looked into the nature of change as well as some of the important concepts of change such as the roles individuals play and the difference between major and minor change. We have also defined the relationship of innovation to change. Understanding these concepts will be important to the development of a template for the cycle of change.

Suggested Exercises

1. Do you agree with Arno Penzias' definitions of invention and innovation? Explain your answer and give examples.

2. What is the significant difference between the role of the sponsor and advocate? Why is this so important?

3. Ask a group of project managers to identify the names of the individuals who played the roles of sponsor, target, and agents. Were there projects in which none were clearly identified? Were the project team members aware of these roles?

4. Describe major change in your own words. Why is it important to be able to recognize major change.

5. Describe the culture of your organization (work, school, church). How does this culture affect the organization? Does it make it more difficult or easier to change?

Notes

1. Conner, Daryl, *Managing at the Speed of Change,* Villard Books, 1993, page 74.

2. Conner,   page 78.

3. Conner,   page 137.

4. Conner, I was first introduced to this type of diagram by Daryl Conner at his Edison Electric Institute seminar. Later, my company, Louisiana Power & Light, had him for a half day seminar in which he again used this diagram which I found to be very useful in trying to understand the relationship between culture and change initiatives.

5. Conner, Chapter 7.

6. . Spann, , M.S., Adams, M., Souder, W.E., Bowen, D.M.,and Sioukas, A., *Measures of Technology Transfer Effectiveness: Key Dimensions and Differences in Their Use by Sponsors, Developers, and Adopters,* IEEE TRANSACTIONS ON ENGINEERING MANAGEMENT, Vol.42 No.1, February 1995.

7. Gehani, R. *Management of Technology and Operations,* John Wiley & Sons, Inc., 1998, pages 142-143.

8. *Fast Talk*: *The Innovation Conversation,* FAST COMPANY, July 2001, page 74.

Chapter 2

WHY CHANGE?

"If it aint broke, don't fix it"
Anonymous

The question "Why change?" is a legitimate one which each person or group should ask and answer before attempting a major change. The old adage "If it aint broke, don't fix it" has come under criticism since the Quality movement. The Quality movement implied that to continuously improve and stay competitive, we should change even if everything seems to be properly functioning. However, this very same Quality movement has presented us with some conditions in which change is not beneficial. A case in point is W. Edward Deming's two causes of variation. Deming says that variation, which he considers one of the primary causes of poor quality, comes from two cases, common causes and special causes. He defines special causes as those that come from external sources that are not inherent in the process. Common causes are those "normal" variations which are observable in a stable process and which can be predicted statistically. Deming claims one of the major tasks of management is understanding what a stable system is and knowing the difference between special and common causes. He says that management needs this knowledge because if they "tinker" or otherwise attempt to change an already stable system, they not only cannot improve the system but may degrade it.[1]

Another reason not to change is that the organizational culture may not be able to sustain major change. Any change would have to be in small increments until the culture is better prepared for radical change, which is best undertaken when there is a consensus that the company must change to survive. In other words, it must be a business imperative. If there is not a consensus backing a serious need to change, it will probably fail. Similarly, change should not be undertaken simply for change sake, that is, just because everyone seems to be doing it. The decision to change should be a reasoned one.

Some successful companies have actually done well by avoiding radical change, such as re-engineering. Nestle, a 134 year old company founded in 1867 in Vevey, Switzerland, has been extremely successful and has a policy of avoiding radical change. In fact, it has a document that identifies those aspects of the company that should not change -- its "untouchables." Peter Brabeck, the CEO of Nestle, acknowledges that all companies must change in order to compete in today's turbulent marketplace, but he contends that they must not change everything all the time. He believes such an approach is unsustainable for the business and devastating to the people operating it.[2] It is management's responsibility to decide whether or not to change and how much to change. However, what Braback may be implying is what some call "pacing," which essentially means to change at the rate in which your company can assimilate change.[3] Rather than not changing, Nestle and others have determined that any change must be something they can assimilate and institutionalize. Otherwise, they elect not to change until the company is ready.

We have begun with potential reasons as to why someone should not make radical changes even though most would agree that incremental change such as continuous improvement is necessary. Pointing out that not all companies should undergo radical change is done on purpose because with so much being said and written about the importance of change, it should be made clear from the outset that there are some legitimate reasons not to make radical changes. Having said that, then what are the reasons to change? To begin with, change is natural. Our growth as individuals and organizations are the direct result of change. Without change, we can often find ourselves and our organizations out of the race. In fact, to address this, a whole body of knowledge has developed linking self-organization or self-generation theory to business organizations. Self-generation theory, sometimes known as chaos or complexity theory, had its beginnings as a revolutionary new way of understanding how natural systems work. Of particular interest were those systems which seem to flourish despite major changes in the environment in which they operated. It was believed that if we could replicate these self-generation characteristics in our organizations, then we could create organizations which can continually stay competitive by continually reinventing themselves.[4] This is certainly a strong argument to change. Simply put, change is necessary to keep up and radical change is often required to stay ahead of the competition.

Environmental Scanning and Vision

Knowing whether or not to change depends largely on the vision of your company and its ability to do good environmental scanning. Environmental scanning, while usually associated with external scanning, also applies to looking inward. Unfortunately many companies who have a very good history of success are often the ones who fail to recognize the need for change. Some retail stores who were very successful in their locations on main street thought the new suburban malls were not important to their success. Some main frame computer companies failed to realize that the personal computers were not just for home entertainment. Even if they were doing environmental scanning, their past successes blinded them to the fact that the competitive environment had changed dramatically.

It should be no surprise that the more established companies are the most difficult to change, even if they have done environmental scanning. The inability to change that most corporations face as they mature is the result of what Richard Foster, author and partner in McKinsey & Company, calls cultural lock-in. He uses the example of how Johnson & Johnson overtook Bayer aspirin with Tylenol. Sterling Drug, which owned the Bayer brand, had a strong culture backed by 50 years of success. Bayer showed typical signs of the mature corporation. It was concerned that the introduction of its own non-aspirin pain reliever, Panadol, might adversely affect its market for aspirin. Bayer had all of the same information that Johnson & Johnson had about what the market was doing, but its culture prevented it from acting on that information.[5]

Companies, like people, follow stages of emotional growth. In the early years, companies are passionate risk takers. As they mature, their culture often prevents them from changing. Even when environmental scanning provides indications of major change in their industry, the mature company often claims that it does not affect them and, instead of accepting change, continues to develop strategies to protect existing businesses.

Environmental scanning should reveal two areas of importance to your company. These areas are either potential problems or opportunities. Either may be a reason to change. The problem revealed could be the realization that you will be in serious trouble if you do not change quickly. It could be a major shift in the market in which you have lost your dominance or may even relate to your organizational survival. Deciding to change in this case is relatively easy, since it is a change or die scenario. Decisions on opportunities which surface as a result of the scanning are often more difficult, primarily because failure to act only means a missed opportunity rather than survival. However, it is important to look seriously at each opportunity because taking action on these types of opportunities is what usually keeps a company growing and remaining competitive.

If the environmental scans reveal no problems or opportunities, or if existing management, as noted above, does not recognize the problem or opportunity, then any possible changes may have to come from the vision of the company leaders. For example, if you have a new product or process ready from R&D, then this may present an opportunity to change the market environment yourself and become a "first mover." This, like the opportunities resulting from environmental scanning, is usually a more difficult decision but these are the types of changes which make industry leaders. A good example of a company not recognizing the problems and opportunities from their own scanning, but was recognized by their leader, can be found in a story told by Jack Welch, the CEO of General Electric.

It was in 1981, and Jack Welch was visiting the nuclear power group. Nuclear power had been one of GE's big ventures in the 1960s and had attracted some of the best and brightest in GE to their San Jose location. Unfortunately, two years earlier the Three Mile Island reactor accident had put an end to what little public support there was for nuclear energy. During the two-day review, the nuclear power group management team presented a rosy plan, assuming orders for three new reactors a year. They saw the Three Mile Island disaster as little more than a blip, their view was completely at odds with reality. The reality was that they had received no new orders in two years and in 1980 their unit lost $13 million. Jack told them that they were not only not going to get three orders a year but stated that he did not think they would ever get another order for a nuclear reactor in the U.S. He told them to figure out how to make a business out of selling just fuel and services to the installed base, which at the time consisted of 72 reactors. They were shocked and tried to bargain with him but he insisted that was what they must do. So they developed a plan in which they eliminated most of their reactor-building infrastructure and focused only on research for advanced reactors in the event the world's view of nuclear energy changed again. The service business became very successful, an early indicator that service could play a huge role in GE's future. This is a good example.

First, this was a business segment that was already in serious trouble and the need for change should have been obvious. Unfortunately their past success put them in a denial mode and not only could they not understand their current situation, but they missed the second point which was the opportunity that servicing the existing plants offered. Fortunately, they had a fresh set of eyes in Jack Welch.[6] Does your company need a fresh set of eyes or a new look at your environment and capabilities? If you don't change, what will your company look like in five years? These are questions which not only need to be asked, but answered.

To Change or Not to Change

The decision to change or not to change must be made by top management. In fact, it may be the go-ahead decision that you want at the end of the initiating phase when you are proposing some specific change which may have come out of the environmental scanning. However, not all need for change comes from environmental scanning. Another on-going corporate activity should be high level discussions about answering such questions as "Should the corporation change?" Why should we change?" "Will the corporation culture support major change?" When these types of discussion are part of the corporate culture they are all helpful in building corporate commitment and sponsorship for the three phases of the change cycle. This chapter has introduced some of the pros and cons of change. Management must ultimately decide whether or not the organization should change. In summary, it is good to get the corporation involved in general discussions about change prior to advocating a specific change. If the corporation sees no need for change, then it should not be surprising that your proposals for change are ignored or denied. What this usually means is that you have an organizational culture that strongly defends the status quo. This means you do not have the right environment for change and unless you can change the culture, most change initiatives will not succeed. In the next chapter we will discuss the right environment for change.

Suggested Exercises

1. Read the HBR article, Nestle's Peter Barbeck: The Business Case Against Revoluton then discuss whether or not you think that all of Barbeck's improvements were continuous improvement rather than radical change. Keep in mind the definitions of major change.

2. Business core values are often considered "untouchables" when it comes to change. Why does this make sense?

3. Define business imperative. Why is it stated that if the change is major that it should be a business imperative before it is undertaken?

4. On the last major change in your organization, what would have been the answers to these two questions, (1) Why are we changing? and (2) Is this the right change?

5. Why should environmental scanning be a factor in determining whether or not to change?

Notes

1. Evans, James and Lindsay, William, The Management and Control of Quality, Fifth Edition, International Thomson Publishing, 2001, Chapter 9, page 511.

2. Wetlaufer, Suzy, Nestle's Peter Barbeck: The Business Case Against Revolution, Harvard Business Review, February 2001, page 112.

3. Brown, S. & Eisenhart, K. (1998) Competing on the Edge: Strategy As Structured Chaos. Harvard Business Press, pages 161-188.

4. . Lannes, W. J and S. Hartman, University of New Orleans, "The Relationship of Chaos Theory to Innovative Work Groups", Proceedings of the Southwest Academy of Management, Forty-Third Annual Meeting, February 28-March 3, 2001.

5. Foster, Richard and Kaplan, Sarah, (2001), Creative Destruction: Why Companies that Are Built to Last Underperform the Market- and How to Successfully Transform Them, McKinsey & Company, Inc., Audio-Tech Business Book Summaries, July/August, 2001.

6. Welch, Jack (2001), Straight From the Gut, Warner Books, Audio-Tech Business Book Summaries, July/August, 2001.

Chapter 3

THE RIGHT ENVIRONMENT FOR CHANGE

"Change is inevitable in a progressive society."
Benjamin Disareli

Is your corporate culture supportive of change? Some of you will probably answer "yes" and may be correct. Of course, some may also correctly answer "no" and would also be right. If you are about to initiate some major changes, you do not want the answer to be "no". However, "no" may be a great deal better than if your company's verbal answer is "yes", but your company's actions say "no". This is the classic example of not "walking the talk." Unfortunately, this is more common than it should be, and actions always speak louder than words. This is why it is important, when you are trying to decide if your company has the right environment for change, that you look past the company slogans and speeches. You need to take a close look at your company's culture. As indicated earlier, corporate culture is based on behaviors; it is the way we do things. For example, some companies may say "our people are our most important asset," yet they do not provide resources or time for training and educational programs. Clearly this type of company is not "walking the talk" in regard to their people. What is probably most disturbing is that companies such as these often continue to claim that their people are their most important asset. Their claims are often convincing until you look at their actions. You need to look at your company's actions, you need to look at the way you do things; you need to look at your culture.

Your company culture plays an important role when you are considering major change. Many companies say they are in favor of change, but when you examine their culture, you find that new ideas are given little real attention and there exists "the old established way is always right" mentality. This type of environment lacks the openness to encourage and support change. I recently had a discussion with a manager of very large construction projects. He indicated that if he assembled in one room all of the construction companies with whom he dealt and asked how many believed in "partnering" (the concept in which companies and suppliers develop a strategic alliance to share knowledge, cost savings, and other mutually benefits to ensure future business), he said that they would almost all indicate they believed in partnering. After all, partnering is a frequently discussed topic in the construction industry and everyone agrees that it is beneficial. For the construction industry, it is almost a motherhood issue. However, he says that if you then continued your questioning and asked this same group of construction companies how many used only the criterion of low cost to award bids to their subcontractors, they would again almost all indicate they did. The point is that the two questions cannot both be answered "yes". Partnering and low bid awarding of contracts are generally mutually exclusive. Therefore, we have to do more than just ask the question, "is our company ready for change?" We have to examine the culture and the actual environment for change. Other 'clues' that a company's culture may not be conducive to change are such things as: the not invented here syndrome, a strict command and control organization, or an atmosphere of constant "firefighting" because of too many demands on limited resources.

In the previous chapter, the case of Bayer and Tylenol was cited as an example of how culture can keep a company from acting on an opportunity. Bayer certainly thought they believed in change, yet they failed to act. Another example of this problem of inconsistency between saying and doing comes from a personal experience. A colleague of mine from the University of New Orleans College of Business and I were funded several years ago to improve technology transfer in the U.S. shipbuilding industry. The reason for the funding was that U.S. shipbuilding was being asked to bid on more commercial work to make up for the expected fall off in work from the U.S. Navy. Up to that time, U.S. shipbuilding had primarily only one customer, the U.S. Navy. With less Navy ships in the budget for the foreseeable future, the shipyards were being told that to stay in business they would have to supplement their government work with commercial work. This would represent a major cultural change for shipyards. Our original plan was to develop a more effective technology transfer model so that they could more quickly adopt new technologies required in being competitive in the commercial sector. At that time, neither my colleague nor I had a great deal of experience in the shipbuilding industry, so we began with the usual literature search. It was generally assumed that the U.S. shipbuilding industry has been very slow in absorbing new technologies. A literature search verified this assumption. However, we did discover evidence that some shipyards had begun to recognize that the industry needed to become more productive and more competitive on a worldwide basis.

To supplement the literature search and to provide more up-to-date information, we also administered an industry survey and conducted selective interviews. The survey was sent only to U. S. shipbuilders. The survey group consisted of 150 shipbuilders, which varied from small to very large yards. The survey results indicated that many of the key personnel in technology transfer positions in the U.S. shipbuilding industry saw no clear need or direction to change, despite the fact that environmental scanning would have indicated that a great deal of change was happening in their industry, including the U.S. Navy's urging to diversify. As is often the case in research, it became clear after completion of the initial industry survey and interviews, that the original plans needed to be changed to accomplish our goal of providing something useful to the shipbuilding industry. This decision was based on our interviews and some interesting results which came out of the survey. For example, the survey reported that 72% of the respondents indicated that they were doing as well or better than the competition. *Since the U.S. industry only had about 1% of the commercial shipbuilding market, it meant that either the industry did not understand the magnitude of the change going on in its industry or it was an industry in which many organizational members were in denial.* In either case, it did not appear to be an industry which would be receptive to a new technology transfer model, no matter how good it might be. It was then decided that instead of an improved technology transfer model for the shipbuilding industry, what was needed was a method which would be useful in helping the industry do a self-evaluation on how they compared with truly innovative companies. We did receive permission from the funding organization to make this adjustment in the direction of the project and we did go on to produce a self-evaluation method, the Innovation Quotient approach. The Innovation Quotient proved to be quite a good tool for self-assessment of groups or companies.[1,2] In essence, the IQ model was based on characteristics of highly innovative companies and by answering a series of questions the model allowed the group to assess how they scored against the composite innovative company. When assessing your environment for change, you need to sometimes look beneath the stated positions of your organization. You often need a method or a consultant to assist you in looking for the underlying reasons for how you behave as an organization.

The point of relating this experience is twofold: first, to indicate that while some companies may not "walk the talk" by commission, some actually do this by omission. That is, they acknowledge that things are changing, but they conclude that it does not apply to their industry or company. Thus, they do not see a need for them to change despite evidence of a rapidly changing environment. This is most often the problem with companies who have had a history of success and fail to realize that the skills which produced the past success are no longer applicable in the new environment. This could certainly be said of the U.S. shipyards which in the past built some of the finest combatant ships ever (and for that matter still do). But they failed to recognize the skills for being successful in commercial shipbuilding and those associated with building fighting ships, are not the same. They saw no need to change in order to be more competitive in the commercial vessels market.

The second point of this shipyard example is to emphasize how difficult it is to do a self-assessment. Most of us will concede that it is difficult to do self-assessments on ourselves as individuals. Frequently, we seem to have blind spots to our own strengths and weaknesses. To get a good picture of ourselves it is often important to get the viewpoint of an honest friend. This is one of the reasons that 360-degree personal analysis has become so popular. The composite appraisal of peers, subordinates, and superiors will generally give us a more accurate assessment of our individual strengths and weaknesses.[3] The same thing is true for organizations. Assessing your company's ability to change may be one of the situations in which an outside consultant can really help. Tools, such as the Innovation Quotient software mentioned above, and other surveys and questionnaires are available to help an organization assess its ability to change. Fortunately, there are many consultant firms that deal with this and can provide excellent tools and methods for making a correct assessment.

While it is recommended to seek a change consultant who can assist in the evaluation of your company's readiness to implement change, it is also recognized that there will always be those companies who feel that it is important to answer such questions internally and without consultants. It might be helpful for those companies to be provided some of the characteristics normally associated with the right environment for change. They can then benchmark themselves against these attributes. This is similar to what was done in the Innovation Quotient. What follows is a description of those attributes of innovative companies who consider change as part of their culture.

Environment of Trust

Those organizations that are best able to change and adapt always have an atmosphere of trust. This appears to be the cornerstone of all other requisite attributes, which should not be surprising because the literature on the most innovative companies show that they all have a foundation built around trust. Since we have already noted the similarity of innovation and change, we can easily see why trust is so important to the right environment for change. Some of the literature calls this a "no fear" environment, which means people are free to make suggestions without fear of ridicule ("that will never work in our industry!") and are even free to make mistakes without fear of blame (learning organizations).[4,5,6] These organizations believe that if you are not making some mistakes, you must not be trying to improve. This type of atmosphere encourages change, and not just change for change's sake, because these organizations are typically results oriented.

So what about your company? Is there an atmosphere of trust? Are mistakes tolerated? Do employees feel free to make suggestions? Does your company respond to these suggestions? How your company responds to these types of questions will be an indication of whether or not there exists an environment of trust. Trust is an important attribute in organizations which are willing to risk change.

Informal Networks

Companies that foster change and innovation frequently have strong informal networks. What do informal networks do to facilitate change? Well, for one thing, they provide "work arounds" that allow changes to the status quo, which might not otherwise be possible. But they do more than just that. They know how to get things done both within the guidelines of the organization and, when necessary, outside the guidelines. These informal networks are often called "communities of practice" which are loosely defined as the group of persons who know how to get things done. This concept is credited as one of the reasons for the success in introducing new innovations in Silicon Valley. It is mentioned in the book, *The Silicon Valley Edge: A Habitat for Innovation and Entrepreneurship*. A discussion of these networks appears in two chapters, first in the chapter, Mysteries of the Region, and then later in the chapter, Social Networks in Silicon Valley. In reading these chapters, you will discover that these networks do a great deal of sharing that is based on openness and trust. They also provide needed support to keep new ideas alive. Perhaps most importantly, the networks encourage continued attempts at breakthrough change. They engender a feeling that failure is expected in an atmosphere of rapid change and innovation. When a Silicon Valley entrepreneur reports that his venture has failed, the first question everyone usually asks is, "What are you going to do next?" This supportive network keeps the ideas flowing and judging from the success of Silicon Valley where most ideas are successfully commercialized.[7]

In a similar fashion, companies that are very good at innovation and radical change create an atmosphere of opportunity recognition. Research has shown that informal networks play an important role in promoting opportunity recognition internal and external to the firm. The capacity of the firm for opportunity recognition is usually related to the strength of the informal network of individuals engaged in the conversion of breakthrough innovations into new ventures. Informal networks usually take the form of "upward networks," which provide access to senior managers, and "lateral and downward networks," which provide information and confirmation to recognized opportunities.[8]   Companies sometimes try to develop these networks into the culture of the organization. For example, 3M developed the Lead User Process as an accepted company practice which utilized internal and external networks to develop new products.[9] In these cases, the networks may be part of the organization, but frequently function as part of the informal network.

Often, it is through informal networks, not just through traditional organizational hierarchies, that information is found and work gets done. However, not all companies are as forward thinking as 3M and many companies treat informal networks as an invisible enemy. They believe the informal network keeps decisions from being made and work from getting done. [10] If you have an informal network and it is used in this way, then it may not be helpful in implementing change. When considering change, it will be useful to determine if you have an effective informal network and determine whether or not it supports change initiatives by reducing or circumventing organizational resistance. Does your company have an informal network? Does it support change through a "can do" spirit through actual work-arounds or does it merely provide information as to what is happening within the company. An effective informal network creates an environment that allows change to happen.

Metrics Are Important

If your company is interested in the potential results change will bring, then there must be some means of measuring the results. Only those companies who measure results are true change advocates because those companies are interested in improvement. How else do you know if you are improving unless you measure? This does not imply that companies that do not have standard corporation measures (balanced scoreboard, etc.) can not be successful in change, although measuring the current situation assists in knowing what needs to improve (change).

How does your company track new initiatives or the introduction of new products or processes? Do they require measurable outcomes? Are individuals or groups who advocated the change held accountable for results? Are there post-project meetings that result in further actions? Does the company have an active "lessons learned" policy? Note that, in a trusting environment, these results are used for learning and improvement, not for blaming. These activities are all signs that the company is interested in constant improvement and, hence, change. It also means that they check or measure outcomes. Further, this measuring is often part of a company culture that requires the use of a continuous improvement processes such as the Shewart or Deming cycle (Plan, Do, Check, and Act). Metrics are required for the check phase of the cycle. Does your company have a continuous improvement policy? If so, in the check phase how does it measure results? The answer to this question will provide additional input as to whether or not you have the right environment for change.

An Environment for Empowerment

Companies that have a good environment for change empower their employees. Empowered employees are a powerful catalyst for change. The problem is that many companies do not understand empowerment. In fact, empowerment is often another good example of not "walking the talk." Many companies say that they empower their people but do not actually transfer the authority to make the necessary decisions. Many in management say they are for empowerment but actually do not practice it because, despite the fact that they believe it makes the company more effective, they are fearful of losing some of their "power." In addition, some companies think empowerment simply means allowing your employees to give input before management makes the decision.

Empowerment has to do with moving the decision level to the lowest level of competence. This is where the efficiency and effectiveness comes; this is where change is generated. It involves transferring the "power." Without a transfer of power, there is no empowerment. Because an empowering environment is so important to successful change, we will spend some time defining empowerment so that you can recognize whether or not it exists in your organization.

Defining Empowerment

The concept of empowerment is something broader than the traditional concepts of delegation, decentralization, and participatory management. Empowerment assigns to the manager of frontline decisions the authority and responsibility for the entire job. It is the issue of power that differentiates empowerment from earlier approaches to employee participation that tended to emphasize employee input but made no real change in the assignment of power and authority.[11] Something that is often not understood by management (and may be one of the reasons that some will not embrace empowerment) is that *only competent employees can be successfully empowered.* This is the safeguard against "letting the lunatics run the insane asylum," which, unfortunately, is the way some management feel about empowerment. In truth, they have a point. If your company is full of employees who are not competent, you should not empower them. This means that only companies who have highly trained and educated personnel can successfully implement empowerment. Companies who value their employees and support them through training and resources are often the best at empowerment.

Empowerment is a management style in which work responsibility and authority are assigned and explicitly accepted. To more fully understand empowerment, it is helpful to recognize that it takes two parties for empowerment to happen. The two parties are the assigner (the person transferring the power) and the assignee (the person who is empowered to do the work). Understanding their roles and responsibilities will help you understand the empowerment process as well as to help you recognize empowerment in the workplace. The assigner and assignee accept a set of principles of behavior, which are basically defined by their joint responsibilities: the assigner responsibilities, and the assignee responsibilities.[12] They are indicated below:

> Joint Responsibilities (assigner and assignee):
>
>> 1. Defines the boundaries of the work,
>> 2. Identifies the resources needed,
>> 3. Agrees on the goals, that is, what is completion and success.

Assigner Responsibilities:

1. Manages the boundaries (<u>not</u> inside the boundaries),
2. Accepts the responsibility to clearly define the work,
3. Acts as a coach/mentor, if required,
4. Avoids intervening in the details of the work.

Assignee Responsibilities

1. Puts together the work plan,
2. Works the plan,
3. Reports progress,
4. Manages the team/project (controls costs, etc.),
5. Solicits help from the assigner, if and as needed.[12]

Listing the responsibilities brings up another important and frequently misunderstood characteristic of empowerment, namely the concept of boundaries as a means of setting limits on empowerment. *Setting limits on the type and amount of empowerment is the process of setting boundaries* and is similar in importance to the precept that only competent persons can be empowered. In fact, competence is one of the factors in establishing boundaries. Boundaries are established by the tasks to be accomplished as well as by the competencies of the assignees. In addition, managing the boundaries is considered by me as the new primary task of management. Understanding this helps managers to realize that they have not lost power, but rather their responsibilities have changed. These new responsibilities are actually more in line with traditional management roles.

The necessity of setting boundaries means that empowerment is a matter of degree, rather than an absolute. Once managers understand this, they can become more comfortable with the implementation of empowerment. Managers are free to choose to provide higher degrees of empowerment to some individuals and teams doing certain tasks than to others since the setting of boundaries depends both on the task and the competency of the team. In setting boundaries it is necessary to understand that there are two types of empowerment, content and context.[9] Content is usually associated with the "how" of the task assigned. For example, empowering someone to come up with the standards in their primary area of expertise (competency). Context is generally associated with the "why" of the task under consideration. For example, if the group or individual was empowered to decide whether or not the company needs standards in the first place, they would be empowered in context.

If your company already incorporates empowerment as a means of being more effective, a careful examination of most companies will show that most empowerment happens in the content arena. This is, of course, not bad since allowing the persons with the know-how to make decisions in his/her area of expertise is an excellent way to improve the effectiveness of your workforce, and, hence, your productivity. However, the changes, which produce the best results on your company's competitive advantage, occur when the teams are empowered in both content *and* context. These teams are usually referred to as self-managed teams. This is the highest form of empowerment and also the most effective.

The Ultimate Environment for Change

Consider, if you will, an organization that changes itself to match the changes in the environment in which it functions. Such an organization would be self-perpetuating and would be ensured of its survival by remaining forever adaptable. Do such organizations exist? Yes, primarily in nature, and they are called self-generating systems and are very similar to the self-managed systems discussed briefly in the empowerment section. Examples of self-generating systems that appear in nature are animal species which continual adapt to their changing environment by changing themselves to insure their survival. This is true of not just individual animal and plants but eco-systems as well. For example eco-systems that continual change as their climatic environment changes are considered self-generating.

In recent years, there has been a tendency to describe groups which have the ability to not only survive but also to excel in terms of the self-generating groups found in nature. A self-organization or self-generation system is capable of renewing itself. It is important to note that the renewed form may not be anything like the original state and, therefore, represents a major change. From an organizational standpoint, however, this ability to renew or successfully go through a major change is perhaps the most desirable characteristic of chaotic systems. If we can create self-organizing systems and organizations, then we know that we will have a system that can continually stay competitive by continually changing itself.

Self-organization or self-generation can be best understood by the study of chaos theory, which emerged from studies in meteorology, fluid dynamics, mathematics, and others. It was later that it began to be applied to natural systems, such as fish populations and then even to applications in social systems, including organizations.[14] It should be noted that when applied to social systems, chaos theory is often referred to as complexity theory. Although the terms complexity theory and chaos theory are often used interchangeably, complexity theory is most often linked to studies of organizations and little mention is given to its roots in chaos theory.

Chaos theory deals with non-linear systems and employs a unique set of terms to describe its relationships. Some of the terminology of chaos theory is confusing, to say the least. Such terms as strange attractors, bounded instability, and SDIC (sensitive dependence on initial conditions) are enough to ask ourselves: does any of this make any sense and, more importantly, how will this help my understanding of change? This is, of course, a legitimate question. So let us begin by trying to relate some of these unusual terms to organizations.

Even though we are dealing with organizations, the term chaos theory will be used in this book. Remember the purpose of introducing chaos theory is to introduce the concept of organizations that are capable of renewing themselves. While we will introduce some of the concepts of chaos theory to better understand self-renewal, the interested reader should refer to the many good references on chaos and complexity theory at the end the chapter if the reader wishes to develop a better understanding of this subject. For the purpose of an introduction to chaos theory, we will define some of the terminology in relation to organizations.

In regard to organizations, some say that *attractors* are equivalent to organizational culture and the way that culture handles feedback. For example, if the culture is not open to change and uses negative feedback to force any change back to the equilibrium position, then the organizational culture causes the behavior to resemble a linear system associated with a *point attractor.* This type of organization will struggle to stay competitive if operating in an environment where breakthroughs or leapfrogging are needed. On the other hand, if an organization encourages change and provides positive feedback, it has potential to be creative and will most likely reinvent itself continually. This type of organization is *non-linear* and has behavior which resembles what chaos theory calls a *strange attractor.* Organizations where feedback is positive, but is used inconsistently or at relatively low levels, may have spurts of creativity but will not produce breakthroughs, a situation analogous to the *limit cycle* in systems.[15] Perhaps to better understand these terms let us consider the case of a marble in a large cup place on a potter's turning table. If the table turns very slowly, the marble will settle in the bottom of the cup and if viewed from the top, the marble will appear as a point even though the table is turning. This would be equivalent to a *point attractor.* Let's suppose that we speed up the table until the marble is spinning around and is in sync with the spinning table. The marble will be spinning around at some specific level in the cup and stay there since the speed of the table keeps it at that location. If viewed from the top, the path would appear as a circle and would be equivalent to a *limit cycle.* Lastly let's speed up the table so fast that the cup begins to wobble. In this case, the marble will take an unpredictable path and if we viewed this form the top it would appear as near random paths in which the same path was never taken and would be equivalent to a *strange attractor.* This last stage would be considered far from equilibrium. Note at this stage it is close to the boundary of chaos. If there is too much wobble, the marble will be thrown from the cup which would be the equivalent of becoming chaotic. With a little less wobble, the marble will stay in the cup but its path is not predictable.

Far from equilibrium, or bounded instability, is the condition in which systems that are governed by *strange attractors* find themselves. This is a desired condition because it is under the condition of bounded instability where new and unpredictable things can happen. This is the most creative place to be, and the area in which change is most likely. Because it is both bounded and unstable, the implication is that the system itself is close to the boundary between chaotic destruction and chaotic self-generation. If too much positive feedback is applied, the system could be destroyed. It is important in both the natural world and in organizations to avoid pushing the system beyond its limits. In an organizational sense, it means that we have to *manage the boundaries*, which is the role of management in creative organizations. Because the far from equilibrium condition is close to the boundary between chaos and bounded stability, it is not only an area of creative reinvention but it is an area of creative tension. This condition leads to the positive use of tension and conflict to create and generate new perspectives. Here there is a need to orchestrate, rather than balance, the extremes which result in this creative tension, another condition which describes creative organizations.[16]

Chaotic systems are non-linear systems and are both sensitive and depend upon initial conditions. In *non-linear* systems slight changes in initial conditions can result in extremely different results. For example, very small differences in barometric pressure can be the difference in whether or not a major storm will develop. Sensitive Dependence to Initial Conditions (SDIC) is sometimes referred to as the "butterfly effect." This term relates to the chaos theory assertion that the air currents generated by a butterfly today may affect major weather patterns a few weeks later. To predict the future of non-linear systems we have to be able to accurately measure all of the initial conditions. This level of measurement, or even having the ability to determine what the initial conditions *are,* is extremely difficult in natural systems such as predicting the weather. Doing so is even more difficult, if not impossible, in social systems. However, chaos theory asserts that this very *unpredictability* is a positive rather than a negative. We know the system will produce changes; we are, however, uncertain of the change.

When applied to organizations, it is this sensitivity to initial conditions that allows the organization to constantly reinvent itself. If an organization encourages non-traditional approaches to problem solving through, for example, brainstorming sessions, then the probability of better solutions or completely new approaches is greatly enhanced. Even though we are uncertain as to what the brainstorming session will produce, our experience indicates that some very different outcomes are probable. Organizations that exhibit characteristics common to self-generating groups will consider change as normal.

Summary

Deciding if you have the right environment for change will require a self-assessment of your organization. Doing a self-assessment often requires assistance from someone outside of your organization. Many consulting firms specialize in this. Once a good self-assessment has been completed, you need to look at the existing culture as described by the self-assessment and decide how different it is from the desired state (the change). Remember, if they are not aligned, successfully initiating, implementing, and institutionalizing change will be difficult, but clearly not impossible. Improving the success rate of change in your organization is what the next few chapters are all about.

Suggested Exercises

1. Give examples of organizations which have excellent value statements and core values but do no "Walk the Talk". What message does this send to employees?

2. Why is an environment of trust so important to organizations who wish to have a capability to change? Can you name companies which have trust as a core value? Why do not all companies have this as a core value?

3.Do you have informal networks in your organization? Describe them, are they helpful or harmful?

4. Why is it important that only competent persons should be empowered? Is this a criteria for empowerment in your company?

5. Understanding setting boundaries for empowered people in content and context is important to the success of any empowerment program. Does your company do this? Which type of empowerment is most prevalent? Give examples.

6. How would you describe your organizational culture; as a point attractor, a limit cycle attractor, or a strange attractor? Explain you answer.

Notes

1 Lannes, W. ; Logan, J. University of New Orleans, Jovanovich, K. Omni Technologies "A Computer-Aided Process for Assessing the Ability of Shipyards to Use Technological Innovation"; Proceedings of the 1997 Ship Production Symposium, April,1997.

2. Logan , James; Lannes, Will; Jovanovich, Kim; Hanlon, Susan: "Innovation, Technology Transfer, and Reward Systems: A Preliminary Study of the United States Shipbuilding Industry", University of New Orleans; Proceedings of the Southwest Decisions Sciences Institute 1997 Annual Meeting, March, 1997.

3. Peiperi, Maury, " Getting 360 Degree Feedback Right", Harvard Business Review, January , 2001.

4. March, Artemis, " A Note on Quality: The Views of Deming, Juran, and Crosby". IEEE Engineering Management Review, Spring 1996, pages 6-14.

5. Kallmeyer, B. (1997) *Re-Engineer the EPC Process,* Construction Industry Institute Report, Research Team 124.

6. Conner, D. (1993) *Managing at the Speed of Change.* New York: Villard Books, page 27.

7. Ford, R. & Fottler, M. (1996) *Empowerment: A Matter of Degree,* IEEE Engineering Management Review, Fall., page 19.

8. O'Conner, Gina and Mark Rice, "Opportunity Recognition and Breakthrough Innovation in Large Established Firms", *California Management Review,* Vol. 43, No. 2, Winter 2001.

9. Von Hippel, Eric, Stefan Thomke, and Mary Sonnack, "Creating Breakthroughs at 3M, *Harvard Business Review,* September-October 1999.

10. Cross, Rob and Prusak Laurence, "The People Who Make Organizations Go-or Stop", *Harvard Business Review,* June 2002.

11. Ford, R. and M. Fottler, "Empowerment: A Matter of Degree", *IEEE Engineering Management Review,* Fall 1996

12. Christopher, W. and Thor, C. (1995),*The 16-Point Strategy for Productivity and Total Quality,* Productivity Press, pages 22-24.

13. Christopher, W. and Thor, C. (1995),*The 16-Point Strategy for Productivity and Total Quality,* Productivity Press, page 21.

14. Hall, N. (1993) *Exploring Chaos.* New York: WW. Norton & Company.

15. Mukherjee, D. (1999) *Validation of Chaos Theory in the Project-Oriented Organization,* Masters Thesis, University of New Orleans.

16. Lannes, W. and Hartman, S., University of New Orleans, "The Relationship of Chaos Theory to Innovative Work Groups", Proceedings of the Southwest Academy of Management, Forty-Third Annual Meeting, February 28-March 3, 2001.

Chapter 4

THE CHANGE CYCLE

"Two roads diverged in a wood, and I,
I took the one less traveled by."
Robert Frost

Change to most of us means dealing with the unknown. And most of us, unlike Robert Frost's traveler, prefer to avoid the unknown. If we can think of change as something known or knowable, we will probably be more willing to travel down new paths. Today we are constantly told that we must embrace change if we are to remain competitive. Yet, we all have difficulty embracing anything we do not know or understand. To overcome this, we must begin to think of change as normal and expected. Indeed, this idea is not foreign to us; we see change in nature with the change of seasons and even witness change in our children as they grow up into adults. For most of us, we are very accepting of these things. These things do not seem unnatural, so, even though we may not embrace these changes, we certainly accept them. For many, we even embrace changes as we experience the joy of our children growing into independent adults or marvel at the changing of the leaves. So if change is a natural process then why is it so difficult for so many of us? Probably because we see it for what it is, it is a change in the status quo, a change that often moves us out of our comfort zone and into the unknown.

Clearly it will be helpful if we see change as normal, like the changing of the seasons or watching our children grown. Before we can accept change as normal, we must understand change. Once we understand something it is no longer an unknown and something to be avoided. Change is, in fact, a very common process in which we move through a transition period from a present state to a new state.[1] The present state is normally not a problem since this is probably where we are most comfortable. And often the desired state is something, which we would really like to happen anyway. What is most bothersome to us is the transition period. This phase of the change process is full of uncertainty and, if not unknowns, certainly new approaches and processes which move us far from our comfort zone. One of the primary purposes of this book is to understand change. Then we will not only accept it, but be able to actually greet it as an old friend with whom we have dealt with on many occasions before. To be successful we must be comfortable with change, because change is inevitable.

Change, for many of us, comes in the form of introducing new processes or technologies into our organizations. This is generally believed to include the following eight steps.

- •Search for available products/processes
- •Screen ideas
- •Feasibility Studies (Technical/Business)

- •Get Approval
- •Develop Pilot Project
- •Test/Evaluate
- •Integrate into business operations
- •Continuous Improvement

Note that these steps are very similar to the seven steps for new product development mentioned in Chapter 1.[2] If we assume we have already selected the idea we wish to advocate then the eight steps can be reduced to six steps (the last six steps in the product development process). But before we look at those six steps let us consider, for a moment, the idea selection step. This first step will have importance in the advocating of the new idea because, if the job of searching and screening is done well, it can reduce the resistance that may occur later. It is probably also important to do a good audit of the current situation prior to the search/screen phase to insure the suggested changes are necessary and appropriate. This will develop buy-in and further reduce resistance.

Now let's go back to the six steps which follow search and screen. These steps can be grouped into three distinct, but related, phases as shown below.

- •Initiating
    - –Feasibility Studies (Technical/Business)
    - –Get Approval
- •Implementing
    - –Develop Pilot Project
    - –Test/Evaluate
- •Institutionalizing
    - –Integrate into business operations
    - –Continuous Improvement

These three phases make up the steps necessary to successfully implement lasting change. In this chapter, as elsewhere in the book, I will refer to these three steps as the Change Cycle as illustrated in Figure 4.1.While we developed the three phases from the steps involved in introducing new products and processes, the phase are very similar to the change model developed by Kurt Lewin. He called his three steps, unfreezing, moving, and refreezing.[3] Unfreezing involves discarding old behaviors from the status quo. Moving refers to the movement toward new attitudes and behaviors. Refreezing is the final step in which the new values and behaviors became the new status, quo, which means that the change has been institutionalized. Recall that in the first chapter we defined change as the transition period between the present state and the desired state. Conner also gives credit to Lewin for inspiring this three step approach to change, although he used different terms to describe the steps (present state, transition state, desired state).[4] The first two phases (initiating and implementing) of the change cycle represents Conner's transition period. Once the desired state is reached it can be institutionalized by making certain it becomes part of the culture. This should make sense to the reader since to successfully introduce the new change into the organization, all three phases must be completed. If we do not institutionalize the change it does not become a part of the way we do things and change does not actually occur. In this case, the new state is never achieved. Recall that the concept of a state indicates some permanence or stability. If the change is not institutionalized, the believed final phase is transitory rather than stable and becomes another " change of the month". That is, the implementation phase becomes the final phase and the transitory nature of the implementation phase means nothing is finalized.

It is also easy to see how the change cycle parallels Lewin's change model. The initiating phase is what we need to do to get people to think about changing the status quo (unfreezing); the implementing phase is what is required to get people to move to the desired outcome of the propose change; and the institutionalizing phase is when the desired change becomes the way we do things (unfreezing). Since Lewin's model has stood the test of time, it is good to see the close comparison between his model and the Change Cycle Model. Lewin's work is well known and while Deming's work in quality in developing the Plan, Do, Check, Act cycle on continuous improvement was done independently, many also see the parallel to Lewin's work in the PDCA continuous improvement cycle.[5]   However, for the purpose of understanding change, I believe the three phases of the Change Cycle Model of initiating, implementing, and institutionalizing best describe the necessary steps for successful change. Fortunately they are also easy to remember, since each phase begins with "I".

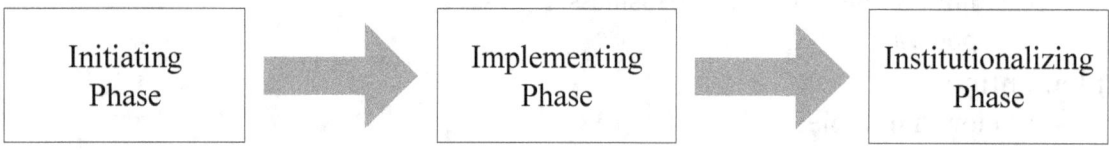

Figure 4.1 The Change Cycle

Let us now examine the three phases; initiating, implementing, and institutionalizing. While these phases are separate and distinct, they are strongly linked to each other. This is one of the reasons we treat the change cycle as a whole; you can not leave out any phase and expect to be successful. During the initiating phase we must be alert to the needs of the implementing phase. During the implementing phase we must know what it takes to make the implementation permanent (institutionalized). Most think of change as only of the implementation process during the transition period. However, if the change from the status quo (present state) is not properly advocated (initiated), there will be no implementation phase. And if during the implementation phase, sufficient attention is not paid to how to make the implemented change permanent, that is, a new standard (institutionalized), then no real change occurs. In this case, the new or desired state is never achieved. Recall that the concept of a state implies some permanence or stability. If the change is not institutionalized, the believed "final" phase is transitory rather than a new stable phase (new status quo) and the initiative becomes, as stated above, just another "change of the month. This is why completing the institutionalizing phase of the cycle is so important. Without institutionalization, change does not endure.

The primary reason for this short chapter is to present the three phases of change; initiating, implementing, and institutionalizing. To be successful you must complete the whole change cycle process. When introducing change into an organization, no part of the change cycle can be incomplete. In the following chapters we will look at each phase individually and develop a worksheet (template) for each phase. However, it is important to always keep in mind the holistic nature of the change cycle process. The three phases are linked and are interdependent. For example, in the initiating phase it will be emphasized that you need a sponsor. The same sponsorship will be needed in the implementing and institutionalizing phases if the change is to be successful. Sponsorship is very important and is essential in each phase. We will see that each phase in the change cycle process has some "look forward" and "look backward" links that are essential to the process and gives the characteristic of being circular or cyclic. An example of a look forward link between the initiating phase and the implementation phase is that you will need to use the project organizational relationship chart to piece together those involved in the project so as to determine *who* is the sponsor, agent, and target. Thus, in doing the initiating phase worksheet you will also begin to answer the first part of the important implementing phase question of *"who* is affected and *how?"* Thus, while the phase of the change cycle process is done in sequence, they are not done in isolation. As you apply this process and gain experience in its use you will begin to more readily see these links and the need to be aware of them in each phase.

As you begin to consider that change is not complete until the final phase of the change cycle is complete, you may begin to muse about changes which were considered or initiated but which are now gone. That is, they did not become institutionalized and become part of your culture, the way you do things. As we complete the next few chapters the reasons for those failures will become more obvious. In fact, after the templates are developed we will ask you to compare some of those very projects to the developed templates. I think you will find that chapter the most useful, but first we must develop the templates. So let us begin the next chapter with the initiating phase.

Suggested Exercises

1. Describe several projects of which you are aware which were never institutionalized. Discuss the reasons as to why this happened.

2. Discuss what you think is the most important characteristic of each phase. What are the links between phases?

3. How would you go about finding out who is affected and how by this change?

4. The three phases of initiating, implementing, and institutionalizing were linked to Lewin, Deming, and the process for introducing new products, which other comparisons come to mind?

5. Discuss the important concept that if the change is not institutionalized, then no change has occurred.

Notes:
1. Conner, D. (1993) *Managing at the Speed of Change.* New York: Villard Books, page Conner

2. Gehani, R. *Management of Technology and Operations,* John Wiley & Sons, Inc., 1998, pages 142-143.

3. Nelson, D. and Campbell, J. *Organizational Behavior,* Thompson-Southwestern, 2002, pp. 622-623.

4. Conner, D. , *Managing at the Speed of Change.* New York: Villard Books, 1993, pp. 87-90.

5. Thamhain, Hans, *Engineering Management,* John Wiley & Sons, 1992, page 384.

Chapter 5

Initiating Change

"Nothing ventured, nothing gained."
Anonymous

All events have beginnings - that is generally accepted. What is often not fully understood are the actions preceding the beginnings. While this may sound strange, it should be noted that in even the simplest cases, we must decide that we will begin something before it starts. So let us look at that decision process. In most companies, and large corporations in particular, projects cannot begin before approval is given by someone in power to allow the proposed action to happen. We have to first advocate what we want initiated to the proper decision maker. Once approved, we can then implement the proposal. Preparing the proposal and getting it approved is the *initiating* phase. While some may not consider this as a separate step, should the proposal not get approved, it will become painfully obvious to them that this step was never completed and the project died right there. So the initiating phase is a very crucial first step and we need to know how to improve our chances of getting past this first step and on to the implementing phase. The first thing we have to do is realize that this step requires as much planning and preparation as does the implementation phase and to realize it is closely linked to the implementation phase.

Some of you may correctly observe that the initiating phase is nothing new. That is true. In fact, you might add that is what you normally do in your budget process. This is certainly a good analogy. You probably prepare numerous proposals (some might say a "wish" list) and then present them to your budget committee or some other oversight group. Typically not all budget requests are approved. For those that were not approved, it means that the initiating phase for those projects was not successful. It is usually useful to analyze why they were not approved. For those that were approved the initiating phase was successful and this gives you one of the first opportunities to benchmark what you did to be successful in your budget meetings against the initiating template (success factors) we will develop in this book. Now that we have defined the initiating phase, sometimes called the advocating phase, let us examine the factors which affect our success or failure during this crucial first step. Remember, while the initiating phase may not be a new phase to some, what will probably be new is the disciplined preparation recommended for this phase.

Success Factors for Initiating Change

When advocating a proposal in the initiating phase, there are several steps which must be taken. By doing each step well, will ensure the successful adoption of the proposal. The steps are as follows:

1. Define the objectives of the proposal.
2. Describe the methodology to accomplish the objectives.
3. Understand how the corporate culture will affect the change.
4. Determine if the proposal represents major change.
5. Determine which parts of the organization will be required to support the change (this will help to determine who the sponsor, agent, and target will be).
6. Follow company procedures and use the appropriate analysis tools for advocating (cost/benefit, etc.).
7. Determine who are the decision makers.
8. Use the language of the decision makers.
9. GET A SPONSOR.
10. Present the proposal.
11. Get approval. [1]

Hopefully, you will look at this list and say that this is just common sense, and, of course, it is. What we will be introducing here is terminology and handy tools which you can put into your new "initiating phase toolkit," which will make it easier to not only carry out this common sense approach but to make it easy to repeat. This will make future proposals easier by following this simple template and it will improve your probability of getting the proposal approved. Let us begin to develop the template by looking at the individual steps.

Preliminary Proposal Planning

The first five steps listed above are all part of the preliminary planning process which the proposer must go through in preparation for preparing the actual proposal. Step one is the most straightforward, but properly defining the objective is important because if the objective is not correctly defined, the follow-on steps can be an exercise in futility. Let us examine some of the steps in detail. In some cases, it will make sense to combine the steps for discussion purposes, keeping in mind there is a great deal of interdependence between the steps.

Objectives and Methodology

Before you define the objectives, it is important to provide a concise statement about why the change is needed, then you define the objectives of the change. When examining why the change is needed it is important that you make the "business case" for the change, that is, how does this help in achieving our business objectives? Defining the objectives of a proposal is generally a given. In fact, in many pre-printed proposal forms for both corporations and funding institutions, there is usually an "objective of the proposal" section. This is usually the section where the problem to be solved or the improvement to be made is described. Because this is such an accepted part of a proposal, we often go mechanically through this section without looking at how the objective may or may not be aligned with the mission or objectives of the company or the culture of the company. Some of the later steps, such as "using the language of the decision-makers" actually address this alignment issue. Describing the objectives in terminology, which is more acceptable to the organization, that is, in the language of the decision-makers, will probably enhance our chances for success. Hence, once you write down the objectives keep in mind that it will be helpful to go back to review and refine them after you have completed the nine steps required before the presentation step outlined above.

Some of the same comments made above about the objectives also are true when describing the methodology to be used to accomplish the objectives. Here we normally describe how the problem to be solved will be addressed. For example, we might state how the root cause analysis will be done to develop a solution. Frequently companies require a section in proposals to list " tasks to be performed" or similar titles, which will require the proposer to provide the methodology. In developing the methodology the proposing organization needs to determine several of the roles related to the change process, such as who will be the agent of change and who will be the target of the proposed change. The agent of change may be an individual or group. In many cases, they may come from a group different from that of the target. Utilization of certain change agents may impact whether or not the proposed change is considered a major change or not. So once again, it may be necessary to review and refine the methodology after the nine steps are completed.

Corporate Culture and Major Change

In the first chapter we mentioned the connection between corporate culture and change. If the proposed change is not aligned with the existing culture, it must be considered a major change and get the proper attention as to planning and sponsorship. Refer to Figure 1 in Chapter 1. Note there is a statement in that figure which warns that changes which are radically different from the company's beliefs, behaviors, and assumptions usually are not successful. For these to be successful, the *corporate culture must be changed first.* Changing the corporate culture is really a major change and more will be said about that later in Chapter 7, which addresses institutionalizing; however, it is important in the proposal stage planning that you recognize whether or not the corporate culture needs to be changed before you undergo the proposed major change. Knowing this may affect how you make the proposal.

Changing the corporate culture on every proposal that turns out to be a major change may not be an option. What other choices do we have? One method is to change the proposal objective so that it will be more aligned with the existing culture but still accomplish most of the original objective. A similar, but better, approach is to look for existing company programs that may exist which could support one or more of the main points of the proposal. This happens more than you might expect and you should be alert to these possibilities once you realize that the proposal, though highly desirable, is almost 180 degrees out of synch with the existing culture. A good example occurred when this approach was used by a senior manager who wanted to change the bid process for a major government agency. He believed that by adopting a strategic alliance or partnering approach with the agency's major contractors, it would transform the agency into a highly productive group. However he realized that since the history of this organization was that it *always* awarded contracts by the low bid process, moving to a strategic alliance approach would probably fail unless the culture was changed first. Hence he began to look for existing programs in his agency that might support some of the main thrusts of his proposed strategic alliances. He discovered that the agency had long ago endorsed a program called "Value Engineering" that advocated some of the principles of partnering. By changing the proposal to advocate using pre-certified contractors instead of using the low bid process he found that the pre-certification process fit very neatly into the value engineering concepts which had already been approved by the agency. In fact, when the Washington, D.C. head of the value engineering section heard about the proposal he strongly endorsed it. Thus, while the senior manager temporarily gave up on the partnering proposal, he was able to accomplish one of his primary objectives, that being to get the agency to seriously consider dropping the exclusive use of low bid contracting. This type of project realignment is related to using the language of the decision makers. By aligning the proposal with value engineering, the proposal was using language with which the decision makers were already familiar. [2]

Another similar example concerned a company which traditionally neglected training. This presented a challenging environment since the main thrust of a new proposal by a productivity improvement multidisciplinary team was to recommend training of personnel as the solution to improve productivity. In fact, the proposal specifically stated that the training should consist of two elements: basic supervisor training and specific craft training. After some discussion, the team agreed that, while there was some movement in the company to recognize the importance of training, it was not yet widely accepted and this proposal would represent a major change. However team members were aware of some new training initiatives that had actually been approved and might fit. Hence, the manager of training was invited to join the team. As it turned out, two new training initiatives fit the proposal quite well. One was a new "pay for skill" type of training program that satisfied the need for specific craft training and the other was an initiative on supervisor training announced by one of the vice presidents. The two programs fit remarkably well into what the team was proposing and it was agreed to align the team requirements with these programs. No longer was the proposal considered a major change because now it was closely aligned with already approved programs. [3]

One more example will be useful for consideration as to how culture and the concept of major versus minor change affect proposals. This has to do with one of the first applications of the principles we are discussing here and it occurred in a classroom setting. I was teaching a graduate class on the management of technology change and we had covered how to successfully advocate change within a corporation. The list of success factors for change we used was very similar to the one in this chapter. At the same time, another professor was teaching a graduate course on accuracy control. Like so many other professors, he and I were both interested in making sure that what the students were getting in class would be useful, particularly in their company environments. So he required his students to come up with accuracy control improvement projects that would apply in their work environments. He and I decided both classes would benefit if a team (2-3 students) from his class would make a technical presentation to our class. Then the following week a team from our class would make a presentation to them on how they should prepare the proposal to get it approved by their company. It was agreed that our team would not alter the technical proposal and could only ask questions for clarification.[4]

The success of this interchange between the two classes was enhanced by the fact that we were both teaching our classes at one of our university's off site classrooms, which was located at an industry site. In both classes the majority of the students came not only from the same industry but the same company. This obviously helped communications between the two teams. The proposal presented by the accuracy control group was to reduce rework by the development of a special team that included accuracy control members in the erection group. During our team's presentation they asked the accuracy control class if they thought the proposal under consideration represented a major change. The initial answer from their class was "no" because the company had had an accuracy control department for some time and since this was an accuracy control project, it was not considered a major change from what was expected. However, our team had been schooled in the concepts of major change and also in asking who was going to be affected by the proposal and how; they began to drill down with their questions. In particular, they pointed out that the proposal would require the forming of a team which consisted of members from two different departments and they asked if that had ever been done before and how would the two departments feel about this approach. As it turned out, everyone agreed that this had never been done before and the accuracy control classes quickly moved to the conclusion that, indeed, this would be a major change and would require a lot of preparation and planning to get all parties on board with this new idea.

The point of these examples is that you must look past slogans and concepts and test whether or not the "talk" is being "walked." That is, while this proposal may be aligned with what we say, the real question is "Is it aligned with what we actually do?" What we actually do is our culture, no matter what our company slogans say. If what you are proposing is different from the way you normally do things, then you must treat it as a major change. The point to keep in mind is that *a change is not determined to be major by the complexity or cost of the change; it depends solely on how different it is from the way we normally do things.* The more closely you can align your proposal with existing norms, the more likely you will be successful. Thus, it may be possible to reduce the change from major to minor if you can align it with existing processes such as was done in the value engineering example.

Developing the Project Organization Relationship Chart

Having decided on a methodology of attacking the problem you need to think about who will be needed on the implementation team or in support of the team to make the change happen. You need to expand from the primary project team into support areas. For example, if this requires a new skill, should training be part of the proposal? Is new equipment involved, does it require special purchasing procedures or can it be handled within the existing purchasing structure? It is quite likely that the project team may be made up of specialists from other departments, brought together in a matrix organization for the life of the project. If this is so, then those departments must be identified and requests must be made for the right resources.

A very helpful thing to do in this step of planning for a smooth initiation of the project is the following: as you begin to identify persons needed in a direct or support role, put that person and his boss in organization boxes. Use "post-um" notes for the organization boxes and attach them on a wall or a large surface. Then determine how they link together. Some may be in the same organization. If so, all of the existing organization chart that is affected should be completed. If the persons and their bosses belong to other organizations, the type of link between these groups needs to be determined. Sometimes these connections can be shown as dotted lines between the organizations.

What you will be developing is a Project Organization Relationship Chart, which can become a very useful visual when trying to determine the target group? the change agent and the sponsor. It is also useful to identify advocates and in which organizations they may be needed. Lets first review the definition of the roles of the various persons first introduced in Chapter 1. [5]

Sponsor: individual or group who has the power to sanction or *legitimize* change.

Agent: individual or group who is responsible for actually making the change.

Target: individual or group who *must actually change*.

Advocate: individual or group who wants to achieve the change but lacks the power to sanction or legitimize it.

The roles should be chosen in the following order: first the target, then the agent, and finally the sponsor. Advocates are in an ancillary role and often the change can be made without advocates (but never without a sponsor). However, in a project with many organizations involved, advocates or sometimes co-sponsors are necessary. The sponsor is chosen last, because depending on who the target and agent are, the sponsor may have to be at a level higher than originally anticipated. Look for example at Figure 5.1 [6] This figure, as well as Figure 1 of Chapter 1 were developed during the class presentation mentioned above. The purpose of the figure was to be used as a brief training and orientation for the accuracy control class before they (the Engineering Management class) led the facilitating for selecting the various roles (sponsor, agent, target). The orientation covered many of the principles developed by Daryl Conner, which have already been covered in Chapter 1. When facilitating a group on initiating change, this type of orientation is essential, particularly when many in the group have no background on the principles of change. When we discuss the use of worksheets in Chapter 8, the necessity of this type of orientation will be revisited.

Relationships

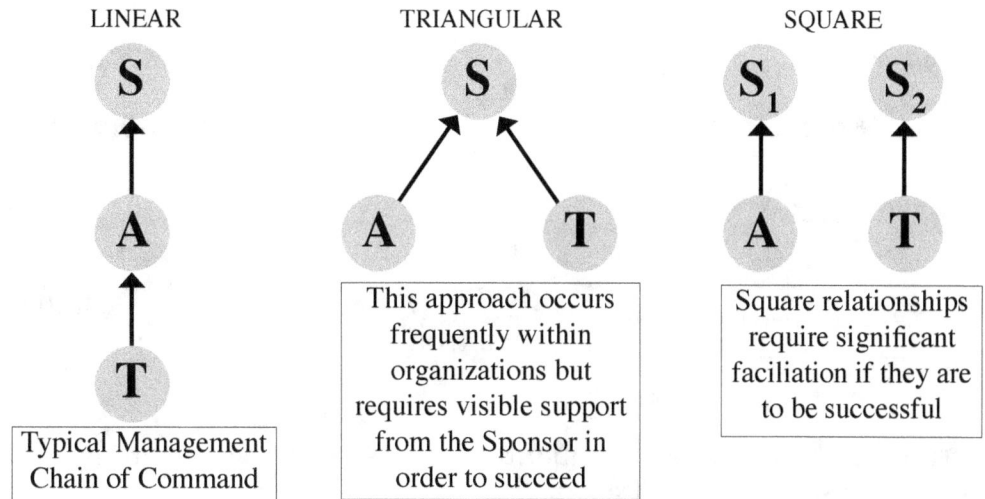

Figure 5.1. Relationships Between Sponsors, Agents, and Targets

Note that there are three basic relationships between the sponsor, agent, and target. They are linear, triangular, and square or box.[7] The most simple is the linear relationship in which the target reports to the agent who reports to the sponsor. Note in the triangular relationship, both the target and the agent report to the sponsor but the target does not report to the agent. This means that more communication is required to be successful in this relationship because the sponsor must inform the target that the agent has the sponsor's authority to provide directions directly to him concerning the change. Without the sponsor's active support, the target may not fully cooperate with the agent because the agent is not the target's boss.

The third relationship, the square, is the most complex. In this case the agent and the target report to two different sponsors who may or may not be at the same level. An example of S_1 and S_2 might be the manufacturing vice president and the engineering vice president. It could also be that the manufacturing vice president and the director of training may or may not be at the same reporting level. In the case of the square, if the two sponsors (S_1 and S_2) are at the same level and are used to working together, then perhaps they could be co-sponsors. Otherwise, you may have to go to the next common higher level and create a triangle over the two main groups involved and request that that person become the sponsor.

You need to create a project organization relationship chart so that you can decide who the sponsor, agent, and target will be. While it is true that you have some idea as to who these persons may be at the beginning of the project, the use of the chart gives confirmation as will sometimes result in changing some of these decisions. This is most likely to happen with the sponsor, which is precisely what the class did when presenting to the accuracy control class. Figure 5.2 is the Project Organization Relationship Chart the students in my class actually used to facilitate the discussion on finalizing the decisions on the sponsor, agent, and target.[8]

Define the roles

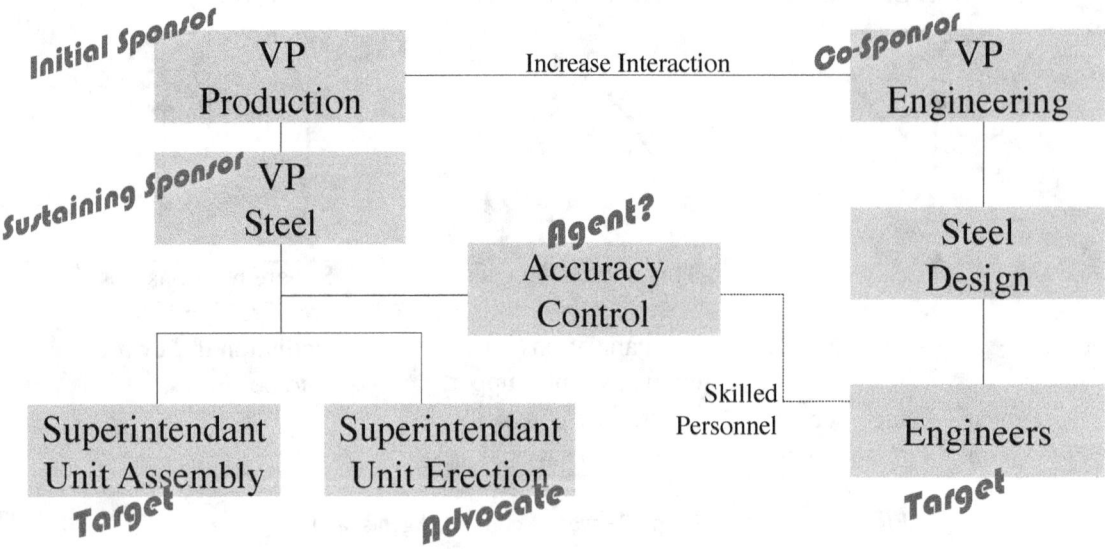

Figure 5.2 Project Organization Relationship Chart

This project organization relationship chart was used to ask the group recommending the accuracy control proposal to select the various roles needed for the change. Once that is done the results can be used for two additional activities. The first has to do with the initiating phase presentation. That is, the group needs to determine who should actually make the presentation. For example, should it be the group that advocated the change, the proposed agents, or perhaps, depending on the approval process, the sponsor him/herself.

It is probably a good time for a brief discussion of the types of traits most desirable in each of the required roles; sponsor, agent, target (adopter). Clearly it is desirable that the sponsor also be an advocate. Not only do you need someone who can legitimize the change but you want some in that position who is enthusiastic about the proposal, some who will "walk the talk" and see the project through to its successful conclusion. If we think in terms of the two entities involved in empowerment discussed in Chapter 3, then the sponsor is the assigner and the agent is the assignee. Recall that the assignee (agent) had to actually implement the task so he must be someone who is skilled in directing teams and in project management. Of the two skills, directing teams is the most important so keep that in mind when selecting agents. The last role, the adopter or target, is often given very little thought. However, the success of the project can be greatly enhanced if the agent takes a good look at his intended adopters. Here is where some of the categories of adopters developed for the successful marketing of new technical products may be useful. The adoption cycle for new technology was divided into the following groups; the innovators, the early adopters, the early majority, the late majority, and the laggards. Clearly it will be important for the agent to identify the innovators. This is the group that wants to be the first to try everything. Are these people out there? You bet they are. Recently, as a user of a America on Line (AOL), I received a notice asking if I was the type of person (an innovator) that wanted to be the first to try new software. If so, they would send me a version of their soon to be released AOL upgrade. Smart companies who introduce new products and processes seek out innovators. Innovators are willing to tolerate mistakes, help fix problems, and, in general, be a willing beta tester. Hence, the agent should first identify those in the group targeted for the proposed change who fit the role of innovator, they will help improve the change initiative and help sell it to the others in the target population (early adopters, early majority, late majority, and laggards). While these terms, which were applied to adopters, are self-explanatory, please see Moore's book, *Crossing the Chasm,* for a more in depth discussion of these different types of adopters. [9]

The second use of the results of the project organization relationship chart is preparation for the implementation phase at which time the details of who is affected by the change and how will be addressed. The project organization relationship chart is an effective tool, not only in determining the roles, but it is useful in answering the question "Who is affected and how?"

Once you have determined who will play the various roles in developing the proposal, the selected agent becomes very important to the next series of steps involving the implementation. The agent must follow the company's procedures and use the appropriate analysis tools to advocate the proposal.

Preparation of the Actual Proposal

The change agent and his/her team that will develop the proposal will need to know existing company procedures for submitting proposals, what type of supporting data or analysis is required, and who the decision makers will be. In addition, the agent will have to understand the language of the decision makers. What this means is that it is important to know what themes, words, or phrases will most likely catch their attention and cause them to be more attentive to the proposal presentation. For example, your company may be going through a major total quality initiative; in that case, clearly projects and proposals which are supportive of that initiative have a greater chance of success. This is essentially a case of alignment. That is, the agent is attempting to show through language and understanding that what he wants is also closely aligned with the company's main initiatives. Having an understanding of how the proposal you are advocating fits into the company's overall business objectives will enhance your chances of success. This is what was done in the examples concerning "value engineering" and "pay for skills." These were existing programs and, therefore, were already aligned with the business objectives.

The Decision Makers

At first glance it might seem easy to identify the decision makers, and, in fact, it often is. Typically, the decision maker will be the sponsor since he is the one who can legitimize the change. However, there are often cases in which the decision maker will not make a decision unless he checks with some in-house expert. This often happens in specialty areas such as information technology (IT). For example if the decision is about purchasing some new enterprise software, the president will often not agree unless he checks with the vice president of information technology. What this means is that although the Vice President of IT does not have the power to legitimize the project, he does have *veto power*, these persons are called Influential Advocates. Consequently, the person advocating some important IT project must ensure that the person or persons with veto power is given as much (and sometimes more) information about the project as the ultimate decision maker so that the person with veto power can evaluate it and support it.

Another example of recognizing decision makers with veto power, the Influential Advocates, is when there is a long chain of command to go through to get a decision. For example, suppose a manager who wishes to get approval for a proposal must go first go through his director, who then has to go through his vice president, who then ultimately takes the proposal to the president for a decision. This is depicted in Figure 5.3.

Figure 5.3 Chain of Decision Makers with Veto Power

The chain of decision makers with veto power often will make the approval process much more difficult. It requires a great deal more of persuasive communications than might be normally required and, in essence, requires that you treat each person in the chain of command as both a sponsor and an advocate. Each one in the chain will have to advocate for you at the next level. This means that you need to make every effort to impart all of the required information to those in the chain so that they can advocate the proposal as well as the originator of the proposal might. Unfortunately the opportunity for misinformation is high and frequently this is manifested when a question is asked by the ultimate decision maker and the person with veto power cannot correctly answer, but the originator of the proposal could have. The worst result of this situation is that the proposal is rejected, the best that can be hoped for in this situation is that the decision is withheld pending additional information which you can provide. The best outcome when a chain of command exists with several persons empowered to veto the proposal between you and the decision maker is to get permission for the originator to make the proposal to the ultimate decision maker. The important thing to remember when determining who will be the decision maker is to make sure that you also include all possible persons with decision veto power. Without considering them, the proposal may not get off the ground. Persons with veto power can be a staff person, such as the Vice President of IT, or it can be a line person in the chain of command.

Language of the Decision Makers

Now that we have decided who might be the decision makers, let's consider what types of ideas or statements will most influence them. They will certainly be more tuned in when ideas or statements related to their "hot buttons" are addressed. In addition to understanding what are the topics of most interest you need to understand what formats and language are they ost comfortable. You need to know the language of the decision makers.

It is possible you are thinking that we are a small company and really do not have any special procedures – we simply ask the boss. In addition, to being small, you may not believe you have any major company initiatives or "special language". Even if that is so, there is one common language which all decision makers speak, and that language is money. In fact, we can take a lesson from some of the early leaders of the quality movement about this "language" problem.

J. M. Juran was one of the early giants of the quality movement. He knew quality could help productivity as well as the bottom line of every company, but he was having difficulty getting top management to adopt quality. Although Juran knew his analytical methods could identify areas needing improvement and could help make and track changes, they were in the language of the shop floor: defect rates, failure modes, not within spec, and the like. Juran recognized that such measures were not likely to attract top management attention; for this reason, he advocated a cost-of-quality (COQ) accounting system. Such a system spoke top management's language— money. He begin to equate such events which were the result of poor quality, such as rework and warranty work, to actual costs. He developed a series of groups of costs due to the lack of quality.[10] They are as listed below:

•Internal failure costs : scrap, rework, retest, downtime, yield losses, etc.
•External failure costs: complaint adjustment, returned material, warranty charges, etc.
•Appraisal costs: incoming materials inspection, inspection and test, maintaining test equipment, etc.
•Prevention costs: training, quality reporting, etc.

With his cost of quality language, Juran began to win many converts to his quality methods. His cost of quality was essentially a means of communicating: "If you do not adopt my quality proposal, here is what it will cost you." Management understood that. You need to do something similar, that is, to develop your proposal so that it quantifies in dollars what the company will lose or fail to gain if the proposal is not adopted. In addition, your proposal can be strengthened if you use other language that represents at least the "hot buttons" of the management team making the decisions.

While money may be the universal language of management, it is clearly not the only language and sometimes major initiatives, which might be undertaken by your company such as LEAN manufacturing, Total Quality Management, and others, might be a stronger "language" than just addressing cost and profit. Showing how your proposal supports, for example, the company's Total Quality initiative may improve your chance of approval more than the fact that the proposal could improve the company's bottom line. That is because TQM is the company's "hot button." Sometimes the language of the company may be more subtle (and sometimes less positive) such as when downsizing is the company initiative. If you can show that your proposal of adopting the new technology will result in a gradual reduction of staff through normal retirement, while also improving productivity, the probability of getting approval will go up.

Speaking the language of the decision makers is just another case of alignment. When we say we are speaking the language of the decision makers we are saying that our proposal is aligned with the company's initiatives and mission. Again, this was the case in the previous example when the engineer changed his proposal from "partnering" to "value engineering". Alignment is one of the most important factors involved in the successful introduction of change into organizations.

Getting to Yes

In this chapter we have developed some tools for consideration and use when preparing to introduce some new technology into an organization. The tools are meant to be a guide or checklist in the preparation of the proposal. Before you get approval of your request you must first make the proposal. This may be as simple as asking your boss, in which case, you will have all of the check list in your head in order to answer any possible questions; or it may be as complex as an elaborate PowerPoint presentation to the Board of Directors. In either case, if you address the steps outlined in this chapter, you greatly increase the probability of getting a YES!

Suggested Exercises:

1. Examine a past project of your group and determine who were in the key roles of sponsor, agent, and target. Were the roles apparent to everyone on the project team?

2. Discuss a project that is presently being initiated, develop a project organization relationship chart for the project. Who will be the sponsor, agent, and target? Discuss how the development of the chart was helpful in correctly identifying the roles.

3. Think of examples in which an *Influential Advocate* had a direct affect on the decision maker (hint discuss mom and pop companies first).

4. Discuss how the relationships of the persons filling the roles of the sponsor, agent, and target are affected by the place in the organization. Begin with the common relationships discussed in this chapter (linear, triangle, square), are there other possible basic relationships or are they all combinations of these three cases?

5. Discuss the procedures in your company for getting proposals approved. How are they affected by some of the factors discussed in this chapter?

Notes:

1.This list comes from my lecture notes from my course on managing technology change.

2. Accarado, Chris, *An Evaluation of the Effectiveness of Awarding Construction Contracts Solely on the Basis of Price with a Focus on the Procurement Practices of the United States Army Corps of Engineers, New Orleans District*, University of New Orleans Thesis for Master of Science in Engineering Management June 2001

3. Lannes, Will and Galle, William, University of New Orleans, *Use of Industrial Engineering Methods to Identify and Reduce Non-Productive Time in the Shipbuilding Process*, Gulf Coast Region Maritime Technology Center Final Report, October, 2001.

4. This occurred in the Fall Semester of 2000 when both classes were being taught at our satellite site in our UNO Center at the Northrop Grumman Avondale Shipyard. The accuracy control course was being taught by our Naval Architecture and Marine Engineering School and the course on managing technology was being taught as part of our Engineering Management Program.

5. Conner, Daryl, *Managing at the Speed of Change,* Villard Books, 1993, Chapter 7.

6. This was one of several PowerPoint slides used in the student presentation for my class (ENMG 6130, Management of Technology Change)

7. Conner, Daryl, *Managing at the Speed of Change,* Villard Books, 1993,

8. This was also one of several PowerPoint slides used in the student presentation for my class (ENMG 6130, Management of Technology Change)

9. Moore, Geoffrey, *Crossing The Chasm,* Harper Business, 1999, Chapter 2.

10. March, Artemis, " A Note on Quality: The Views of Deming, Juran, and   Crosby", *IEEE Engineering Management Review,* Spring, 1966, page 11.

Chapter 6

Implementing Change

"Action is eloquence"
Shakespeare

So your proposal was approved, now what? Sometimes when company representatives comes back from bid openings they will say "Well I have good news and bad news". "The good news is we got the bid, the bad news is we got the bid!" Which is their way of implying that now that they have gotten your YES, they have to take action. Implementation implies action; this is probably why there is so much emphasis on the implementation phase, most of us like action.

While the advocating phase may provide a statement of the method you intend to use to implement the project, it rarely contains enough detail (who will be the team members, what will be the internal milestones, etc.) to spring into action. This is understandable because not only do you not get all of the business on which you bid, but neither do you get all of the items you bring to your internal budget review approved. Hence, it is common to consider resources (potential project team members, etc.) as available for more than one project on the budget list because historically you never get all projects approved. However, once you get your YES, you must quickly put the team and implementation plan together to capture the benefits that were advocated in the proposal.

The implementation phase is often associated with project management. In our action-oriented society, jumping right into managing the project just seems natural. While managing the project is a major part of implementation and very important to the success of the project, it is not what this chapter is about. In fact, we will assume the project manager is competent and skilled in project management and that nothing more need be said. If you need to improve your project management skills I would refer you to the many good texts and seminars on this subject. What we do want to do in this chapter is to provide some tools to address two important questions that are frequently overlooked in the implementation phase. These two questions should be a part of every project management method. Failure to address these questions will often lead to failure of the implementation, which means the change will never be institutionalized.

Before we address those questions we want to also emphasize the importance of pre-project planning prior to implementation. In the last chapter we indicated pre-project planning was important in the initiating phase; it is perhaps of more importance in the implementation phase because of our penchant to rush into action. Taking the time to plan prior to rushing into implementation will pay huge dividends. Many will say that I don't have time to plan; they say, "Once the contract is signed my client expects action!" The same can be said for internal projects. While it is true that many projects are time limited, in general, the more time allotted to up-front planning, the more likely the project can be done in less time. In fact, there is considerable literature which indicates there is a direct relationship between the success of a project and the amount of pre-project planning.[1] So, you need to *make a commitment to pre-project planning,* within the total time allotted even if you are on a very tight schedule. Do not fall into the common trap of saying that I do not have time to plan; make time!

Somewhat along the same line as the importance of pre-planning is the concept of needing a pilot program before full implementation of the change. While this is not always necessary, on large initiatives, it is generally advisable. An alternate to pilot programs is a "paper drill" or training session before the kick off of the actual implementation. This is most often done for operation oriented projects such as undertaken by the military of emergency agencies. Storm or Hurricane drills are quite common on the coast of the Gulf of Mexico. There are ways to test the plan before it is actually needed and a simulated session for training purposes is one of them. Some major construction projects have also included "paper drills" to insert "what if" scenarios to be able to minimize delays once the project is begun. These "paper drills" must be as realistic as possible and must be taken seriously by all participants. Some of these drills should "stretch" the team's capabilities by including worst case scenarios. Katrina, the most devastating hurricane to hit the Gulf Coast in history taught a lot about preparing for worst case scenarios, most agencies were not prepared to execute the plan under those circumstances.

Putting Together the Project Team

Even before we begin pre-project planning we need to first put together a project team. Recall that the key players, perhaps even the project manager, are not usually named until the project is approved because some of those same personnel resources may have been tentatively slotted for several projects which were also up for approval. Hence, the next step, and one of the most important in the implementation process, is to put together a team of key individuals. Good team members can make the difference between success and failure of the implementation. They must be competent and the best available (not just available). Being available is important because they will most likely be matrixed to the team from other organizations and their functional managers must be agreeable for the "loan" of their people, particularly if you are trying to get the best available! This is where the sponsor can be helpful, perhaps necessary. This is just one of the reasons you must maintain sponsorship throughout the implementation phase. Since you will be "borrowing" some of the functional managers' best people, it is sometime useful if you can get some up-front agreements on how the individual will be rated while in your project. This is particularly important if this is to be a rather long project. While this is often difficult to achieve, it can be done. In fact, when I was in industry I was successful in developing a shared rating for pay and promotion with groups which were matrixed to my business unit. If possible, get upfront agreements on the sharing of time of the individuals. This will be a big help when schedules get demanding, and they will! Lastly, I can not over emphasize the importance in making sure the team members are competent. Most successful team use empowerment to attain their high level of success. Remember you can only empower competent people. We will come back to the importance of people in the last chapter.

Recall from the previous chapter that the implementation phase of introducing new technologies or processes into organizations and businesses involves developing the project (usually a pilot program) and then testing and evaluating it. One big problem in introducing new technology lies in determining the *impact* of the new technology on the existing work processes and the productivity of employees. So the first question we need to ask is " Who is affected by this change, and how?"

Who Is Affected and How?

During the development of the project organization relationship chart it was indicated that not only could it assist in determining who are the sponsors, agents, and targets, but that it could be useful in answering the question "Who is affected and how?". One of the first things you should do is to go back to the project organization relationship chart and list the individuals and groups involved in the project. This will generally cover those who are directly affected and many of those who are indirectly affected. However we need to expand the chart concept. Wayne Fisher and Slawo Welsolkowski have suggested a framework which can help. In fact, they have suggested that using this framework for determining the impact of a new technology on all the affected departments and staff in an organization is critical to the establishment of a disciplined, structured, approach to the introduction of new technologies and processes. [2] I believe that this is true. *Many implementation projects get into trouble when they impact individuals or groups which have not be involved in the planning of the implementation.* At best, it can introduce delays as those persons are integrated into the implementation plan. At worst, they can overtly or covertly sabotage the effort because they were adversely impacted but not considered in the planning.

The framework Fisher and Welsolkowski developed answers the question, "Who is affected and how?". They suggest that in order to make sure no group or individual be excluded that everyone be divided into four entities; project management, direct users, indirect users, and infrastructure groups. By placing persons or groups into these four entities you can assess the nature of the impact on each. For example, it may be that some infrastructure group will need additional training in order to make the transition smooth. Without this type of framework, some of these impacts or needs will be missed until the implementation is underway.

They provided some of the general needs of each group which can assist in the assessment you would conduct on your individual projects. These potential needs are shown below in Table 6.1.

Table 6.1 Needs of Direct Users, Indirect Users, Project Management, and Infrastructure Groups.3

Direct Users	Indirect Users
Education on how the technology works	Process Re-design
Education on how indirect user departments will be affected Business Process Reengineering User Training	Knowledge of how changes will affect skill requirements and processes User Training

Project Manager	Infrastructure Groups
Project management	Education on how the technology works
Change management	Knowledge of how changes will affect skill requirements and processes
Education on how the technology works	Technical Training
Tools to analyze changes to direct users	Technical Support
Tools to communicate changes to indirect users	Education on how indirect user departments will be affected

While this tool is very good in making sure no group that might be impacted by the impending change is left out, it still depends on the project team leader's judgment on how much of an impact the change might have. If the change has a large impact them clearly we might expect resistance to the change. How do you judge the impact on the persons affected by the change?

Once it has been decided who will be impacted, the equity implementation model (EIM) can provide insight as to what magnitude of impact we might expect from the change. This was developed by Kailash Joshi and Thomas Lauer and is based upon equity theory, which is a well-established theory in social sciences.[4] Basically it determines if the positive outcomes affecting the person or group impacted by the change exceed the negative outcomes. If the net is positive, change is generally accepted; if negative, change is resisted. Joshi and Lauer look at three different levels of analysis of EIM to determine what type of resistance might be expected and what might be done to address it. The first is what they call Level 1 and looks at the change in equity status for the employee directly affected, which they designated as "self". The second analysis is Level 2 and deals with a comparison of self with the employer and the last level, Level 3, deals with a comparison of self with other employees.

What is required is that you consider both probably outcomes and required inputs to the individual because of the change. There can be an increase or decrease in both outcomes an inputs. For example, in Level 1, Joshi and Lauer provided these possible increases in outcomes are shown below:

More pleasant work environment
Less tension, more job satisfaction
More opportunities for advancement
Better service to customers
Salary increase, grade increase, or higher-level title
Reduced dependence on others
Etc.

Possible decreases in outcomes provided by Joshi and Lauer were:

Reduced job satisfaction
Reduced power
Threat of loss of employment
Reduced importance, control
Increased monitoring and accountability
Etc.

Similarly the increase in inputs could include such things as:

More work in entering data
More tension
Bringing higher level skills to the job
Effort in learning a new system
Assignment of additional tasks
Need to spend more time
Etc.

The decrease in inputs could be such things as:

Ease of usage
Less effort
Reduced manual effort
Less rework due to fewer errors
Etc.

For the complete lists of potential increase and decreases in outcomes and increases and decreases in inputs see *"Transition and Change During the Implementation of a Computer-Based Manufacturer Process Planning System: An Analysis Using the Equity Implementation Model"*, by K. Joshi and T.W. Lauer. While your analysis does not have to be as detailed as that conducted by Joshi and Lauer, it should be fairly easy, from your own experience with your situation, to determine the amount of positive and negative impact on those affected by the change. The important thing is to make sure you give this outcome some attention. It will be very helpful in developing a successful implementation plan. Clearly if the change for the individual is positive (change in outcomes minus change in inputs), then the change will most likely be welcomed. If the change is negative then there will likely be a great deal of resistance. Additional information can be gathered by examining Level 2, which looks at the employer's outcomes. Here is something that is often not considered: if the employee sees all of the benefit going to the employer while all of the work and risk goes to the employee then you can expect a great deal of resistance.

The last level, Level 3, compares the equity between the individual employee and other employees. This comparison is most important when the change results in a shift of workload. For example, when a company decides it will go to distributed rather than central system. Inputs to the system (which previously were done by central staff) may now be required to be done by people in the field (distributed). Most often this is done with no increased help or training for the field personnel and often it is accompanied by a reduction of staff at central headquarters. This represents another inequity with which you must address.

When the question "Who is affected and how?" is answered during the pre-project planning session you greatly increase you chance for success. Going through this drill, with the help of the tools just discussed, will usually result in early discovery of training needs and needs to communicate with individuals and groups who will obviously be impacted but were left out until now. You might even discover the need for some temporary help to assist groups and individuals who have picked up significant new responsibilities but with no budget assistance. This means that you might have to adjust the project budget, for example, to cover training which did not occur to you until you went through the pre-implementation project planning. Discovering these shortcomings before getting into the project will not only save you grief but will greatly enhance your potential for success.

Failure to address the question "Who is affected and how?" could lead to a major disruption of the project and perhaps even failure. Daryl Conner in his discussion on how change affects us says that it is not the surprises in life that are so debilitating; the truly crushing force is being surprised that you are surprised.[5] So if we want to keep surprises out of our change initiatives that we had better answer the question "Who is affected and how?" in our pre-implementation project planning. In fact, the importance of pre-planning is indicated in Construction Industry Institute studies which show that the success of construction projects are directly related to the amount of pre-planning done. So before you activate your implementation plan, take some time to do quality pre-planning.[6]

Capturing the Benefits

The next important question you need to address is "How will the benefits be measured and captured?" The initiating or advocating phase will usually require that the benefits of the change initiative be listed in the proposal. As mentioned in the previous chapter, most proposals will require some sort of cost/benefit analysis. Sometimes the proposal will even mention how the benefit will be measured. However it is only in the implementation phase that the benefits can actually be captured. Why is that? And what do we actually mean by "capturing the benefits".

If the change initiative proposal claimed that cycle time can be reduced by half, or that costs will be reduced by half, or that we will double market share; then we must be able to actually accomplish that during the implementation phase. More to the point, we need to convert that success into dollars and make sure they get to the bottom line. Otherwise, it may be unlikely that the implementation will be institutionalized. Continued success in the implementation phase is what leads to institutionalization and nothing indicates success more than *when a change actually saves money or increases income.*

The history of change management seems to indicate that one of the most difficult things to accomplish is to actually capture the benefits (previously advocated in the initiating phase) during the implementation phase. Everyone is familiar with the constant lament of industry that it is not getting the benefit expected of the billions of dollars they have invested in information technology. Has industry not received any benefit, or are we just not very good at capturing the benefits? Clearly we have received some benefits but obviously we have not done a convincing job to management that we actually have captured those benefits. In many cases, we have not captured the benefits and we and management knows that.

One of the primary problems in trying to capture the benefits are that <u>the savings are not captured at the point of origin.</u>. *If you do not capture the benefits as they occur, they will get lost by the time the project is completed.* So you need to develop a workable plan, which will allow you to capture the benefits as they occur. An example from my own past experience may help to understand this point.

Several years ago I was in charge of all of my company's non-nuclear power plants in Louisiana. We had approximately 20 individual generating units spread out at six primary locations throughout the State. Each year we had an annual outage for each unit to accomplish maintenance and modifications. We scheduled and budgeted each unit separately; however, our president, my boss, was looking for ways to reduce cost of the outages while still getting all of the required work done. One thing he initiated was a procedure for purchasing all needed material for all of the outages with a single purchase order rather than to order material for each individual outage. His belief was that we could negotiate better prices with our suppliers by combining all of the similar parts and material into a single order; and he was correct. One day before one of our outages was to begin, he called me and said " You know that $10,000 worth of "widgets" you budgeted for this outage--well we have just purchased your needed allotment for $5,000". Before I could say that is great, he continued "… so I am taking the $5,000 out of your outage budget".

This was quite a surprise to me because we (and I suspect many of you) were used to moving savings, which we might have gotten in one part of our outage budget to other activities which might be running over budget. However if he had not immediately "captured the benefits" of our new purchasing methods by reducing my budget by $5,000, it is possible at the end of the outage I would have claimed that I finished "on budget" when, in fact, I would have been $5,000 over budget. What is perhaps worse, when the annual outages were over no one would have been able to prove that the new purchasing plan was actually saving money. By removing the savings due to purchasing immediately from my budget at the time the savings occurred, the president actually had an opportunity to roll that reduced cost or savings to the bottom line.

While this is a real world example of capturing the benefits, it is a fairly obvious example involving simply a purchase order with significant savings from the previous manner in which we ordered material for the outages. It did not require any additional tracking systems or complex processes to determine the savings, it simply was a better method of purchasing in bulk to reduce our costs. Moreover, we had the ultimate sponsor in our president who was both an initiating and sustaining sponsor of the new purchasing initiative and insisted that we capture the benefits in a meaningful way. This is what you need to do for your change initiative.

How can this be done? Well there are many ways and hopefully you will be able to come up with a process that is easily aligned with your current work practices so as to make it more acceptable. The first thing you have to do is to develop a plan on how the benefits will be measured. You need to put the benefits into "units of benefit". For example if the benefit is to be reduced labor costs then the unit of benefit will probably be man-hours. If it is reduced cycle time, then the unit of benefit could be minutes or hours. If it is reduced costs, then the unit of benefit will be in dollars. Recalling our earlier discussion that most decision makers in management like to think it dollars, you probably should provide a conversion to dollars if the unit of benefit is other than dollars (cycle time, man-hours, etc).

Once you have defined the unit of benefit, how do you track it? If possible, try to use existing company forms and procedures. One thing I have discovered is that most companies, particularly those in construction and manufacturing, use some form of work order (W.O.s). This typically requires entries on many of the items you might want to be tracking such as man-hours or dollars. For such things as cycle time you may have required "run sheets" or other similar forms for tracking the hours of process or machine runs. These can be used. The idea is that you should first look at existing forms and procedures to see if they are already collecting the measures you want to track.

If you are going to track the benefits, it has to be over a specific time. For example, you may want to compare the man-hours required for certain tasks six months after a new initiative begins to the man-hours required before the change was initiated. This can sometimes be done simply by comparing work orders before and after the change was implemented. The question is what do you do once you have identified the actual savings? Well, if you have an aggressive sponsor like I did when I was in charge of the power plants, he will take care of it. However, I have met very few persons who are tuned into capturing the benefits at all, much less capturing the benefits at the point of origin. Hence you may have to develop a pilot training program which will illustrate how the savings have been captured, but without actually having to modify the existing budgets or processes. This, unfortunately, will require some extra paperwork but will probably be well worth the effort.

What I am essentially advocating is that if you do not have an organization willing to change the budget as events change (such as was done in the example of the newly initiated purchasing method) then you may want to establish a phantom "savings account" for the project. This would at least allow savings to be deposited in the account as they are identified and verified at the point of origin. Developing a fictious accounting system to track savings is not as far fetched as it might seem. Toshio Okuno, the owner of a Japanese Soy Sauce company, developed a Price Control System to be used by each production unit in his factory to track the cost at each step of the process. He even printed fake company money, which was used in the "game" to help workers understand how their actions impacted the cost of the product. This was only one of several methods Okuno introduced into his company to improve productivity and we will return to some of those other methods in Chapter 12 when we discuss the importance of the people who have to make the change work.[7]

Another example, which will be useful in applying this concept of a virtual "savings account" in a real world environment, involved some work I had done with a shipbuilding company. We were looking at improving productivity. One of the things we investigated was reducing rework in the shipfitting area. After doing some root cause analysis, it was decided by the productivity improvement team that the real cause of rework in this area was a lack of training. They felt the training was needed in both craft and supervision skills. Since we were concerned about alignment of the proposed training request with existing company plans and policies, we brought into the team a person from training. Fortunately, that team member was aware that the company was about to initiate a "pay for skills" training program for the crafts. In addition, the company was initiating a supervisory skills series of classes. After consultation with the training team member it was agreed that these two programs, with only slight modification, could provide the needed training for the shipfitting group.

The question was raised in the team "How will we know if the increased training resulted in reduced rework?" Well the first thing was needed was to get a measure of the amount of training and the reduction of rework. Again we discovered that there were in existence two programs with the necessary record keeping which could be used in the tracking. While these discoveries can be considered fortunate, they are often the result of the project team asking a lot of in-depth questions about what is going on in the company before recommending something new. Remember it is important that your implementation plan is aligned with company goals. In this case, they were and we had on the team someone from Accuracy Control who stated that they already had a program to track the man-hours needed for most of the tasks performed in the shipfitting section. It was also agreed that the "unit of benefit" of this intervention (increased training) would be man-hours, actually the reduction of man-hours. Hence the existing Accuracy Control form would be used to track the reduction in man-hours to accomplish the tasks done in shipfitting. In this case, in addition to tracking the "unit of benefit" we also wanted to track the expected cause for the reduction in man-hours, the training. Again the team was informed that Human Resources would have accurate training records on each individual in the shipfitting group. So it was agreed that once management approved of the project that the group would check the improvements at the end of six months using the previously mentioned measurement methods. Additionally, it was agreed since there were no other anticipated major interventions during that observation period, that all improvements (reduction of re-work) would be credited to the increased training. Clearly we had to make some assumptions, but all seemed reasonable and defensible.

The next question the group addressed was, "If our records show we actually reduced man-hours due to better trained employees, how could we possibly capture that benefit"? When the team discussed this there was general agreement that the present culture of the organization would not allow the changing of budgets, the question was asked "What else could be done?" That is when it was suggested that the superintendent of the shipfitting (a member of the team) would keep a separate record of the man-hours saved in what would amount to a "savings account" for the training initiative. Initially he intended to use it as proof to management that the intervention worked and to advocate the continuation of the needed training. Unfortunately for me, my assignment ended before the superintendent could seek approval so I never had the opportunity to see how well the process worked. However, before I left the team there was general agreement among the team members (I was the only non-shipyard member) that the plan to capture the benefits was workable and if enacted could even be improved into a sharing of the benefits between the shipfitting group and the training group. While I did not get to see the end result of their efforts, for the purposes of this book, this is still a good example of how you might go about capturing the benefits in an actual work environment.

In this, and the previous chapter, we covered two distinct, but closely linked, steps in the change process; initiating and implementing. We have provided several tools and developed questions which should be addressed in the process. All of these should be helpful. However there are three questions which are more important than the others. These questions must be fully addressed to be successful in the initiating and implementing phases. They are: (1) Who is the Sponsor of this change? (2) Who is affected by this change and how?, and (3) How will the benefits of this change be measured and captured? If you pay sufficient attention to answering these three questions you will greatly enhance the chance that this change will be institutionalized

Suggested Exercises:

1. Time spent in the pre-planning of implementation activities has been proven to be directly related to the success of the implementation, does your company allow sufficient time to properly pre-plan new implementations? If not, why not? If so, why do you think this is done?

2. Doing a proper " who is affected and how?" analysis is one way to determine the expected amount of acceptance or resistance to the new change, what are some of the other benefits of this analysis?

3. What can the sponsor do to insure that you have the resources the team requires for a successful implementation?

4. The team project leader is the agent for the project, what characteristics are needed for this role?

5. Capturing the benefits seem to be difficult to do and teams seem rarely to be held accountable for achieving these benefits upon completion of the project. What type of post-project review is conducted by your company, does it included accountable for achieving the benefits proposed?

Notes:
1. Kallmeyer, B. *Re-engineer the EPC Process,* Construction Industry Institute Report, Research Team 124, 1997.
2. Fisher, W. and Wesolkowski, S. *Tempering Technostress*, , IEEE Technology and Society, Vol. 18, No. 1, Spring 1999.
3. Fisher, W. and Wesolkowski, S. *Tempering Technostress*, , IEEE Technology and Society, Vol. 18, No. 1, Spring 1999
4. Joshi, K. and Lauer, T.W., *Transition and Change During the Implementation of a Computer-Based Manufacturing Process Planning System: An Analysis Using the Equity Implementation Model*, IEEE TRANSACTIONS ON ENGINEERING MANAGEMENT, November 1999.
5. Conner, Daryl, *Managing at the Speed of Change,* Villard Books, 1993.
6. Kallmeyer, B. *Re-engineer the EPC Process,* Construction Industry Institute Report, Research Team 124, 1997.
7. Copper, Robin and Markus, M. Lynne, *Human Reengineering*, Sloan Management Review, Massachusetts Institute of Technology, Summer 1995.

Chapter 7

INSTITUTIONALIZING CHANGE

"Nothing is more powerful than habit."
Ovid

Institutionalizing a change means that the change has become part of our culture. It becomes what we habitually do. If a change initiative does not become institutionalized, then we cannot really say that change has occurred. We often hear change initiatives referred to as the "change of the month" or "change of the year." This is because the change, even though it might have had initial acceptance, never became part of our culture, part of the way we do things. It never completed the change cycle; it only completed the first two phases and never became institutionalized. Hence, the change is not permanent.

If we do not institutionalize the change, it and all of the efforts associated with the change simply disappear as if it was never initiated and implemented. In a recent article by Susanne Scott and Walter Einstein, I was struck by the opening paragraphs. The article was not about change, but rather about performance appraisals; however, the first paragraphs are a good example of a change initiative that was not institutionalized. The opening paragraphs are repeated below:

> In the early 1990s, a prominent high-tech firm in the northeastern United States enthusiastically rolled out a new performance-management system to improve the performance of its professional work teams. The program was comprehensive, with details contained in two large, beautifully written, leather-bound volumes prepared by external consultants following nearly a year of work. Top management introduced the program with much public fanfare and pledges to implement it.

> Three years after the launch, the second author (Einstein) happened to run into a colleague who was doing research at the firm on the human resource system and productivity: Q: How's the performance management system working? A: What performance management system? The program introduced with such hope had come and gone within the space of a year, leaving in its wake frustration, anger, and cynicism.[1]

Scott and Einstein's article went on to discuss that there is no one appraisal system which fits all organizations (with which I agree). The article implies that was one of the reasons for the failure of the above mentioned implementation (with which I do not agree). The failure was probably more related to the lack of understanding of how major initiatives become institutionalized. So how can we avoid this frustration and cynicism and what can we do to enhance the chances of the change being institutionalized?

We have already indicated that if the first two phases were done correctly, then we increase the probability that the change will be institutionalized. In fact, we said there were three specific questions which should be addressed to improve the chances of successful institutionalization. The first was, "Who is the Sponsor?" Sponsorship is absolutely essential throughout each phase of the change cycle. Without sustaining sponsorship, the change will never become part of the culture. This is probably the most important ingredient in successful institutionalization of the desired change. The other two questions are "Who is affected by the change and how?" and "How will the benefits of the change be measured and captured?"

In addition to these questions we have consistently emphasized how culture affects change. Institutionalization is directly related to the culture of the organization, so let us revisit this concept of culture. Recall from our earlier discussion, culture is the combination of our beliefs, behaviors, and assumptions; it is the way we do things. Culture for an organization is the same as personality for an individual. Figure 7.1 shows the relationship of company culture to change initiatives. In this case let's assume that the initiatives include the 5 S system, Integrated Product and Process Development (IPPD), and LEAN manufacturing.

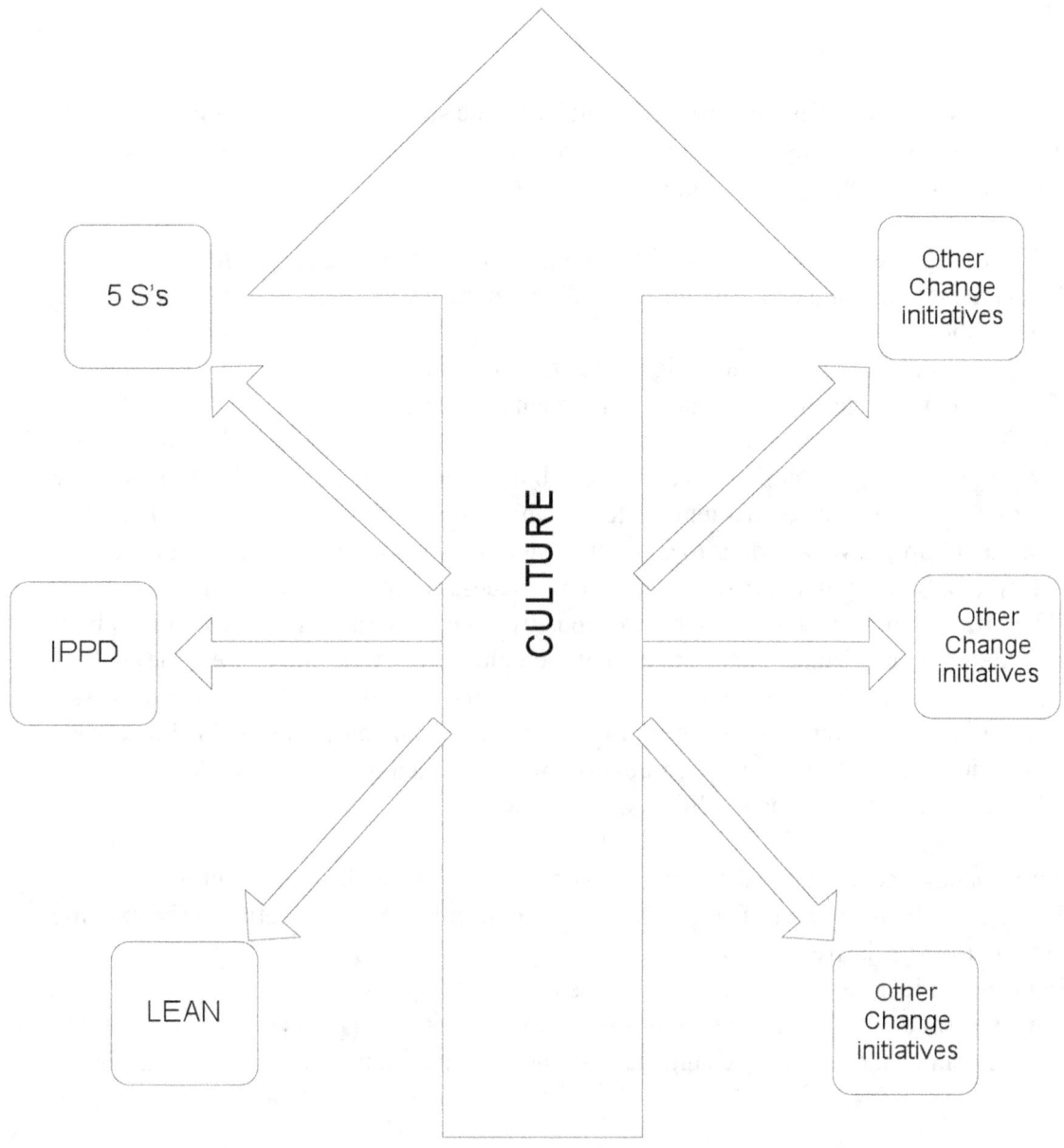

Figure 7.1 Alignment of Change Initiatives and Culture

Suppose the change you wanted to introduce was LEAN manufacturing, but you realize that your culture is such that introducing LEAN would be equivalent to introducing something radically different from the existing culture as indicated by the arrow on the left side of the figure (about 160 degrees our of alignment with the existing culture). However since you know this will be very difficult to introduce you decide that you will first introduce the 5S approach which is a subset of the LEAN approach; 5S is based on getting some order in the shop by (1) sorting, (2) simplifying (3) systematic cleaning (4) standardizing (5) sustaining. This said in simple terms means to "clean up your shop"; that is, a place for everything and everything in its place. Apparently your mother was right! [2]

culture.

The steps articulated by Champy are very much like the steps outlined by Conner in his description on how to change the culture of a company. Conner calls this the Architectural Approach to cultural change. His steps are listed below:

1. Senior management defines the specific characteristics of the desired culture.
2. Management then conducts a "culture audit" to determine the gaps between the existing culture and the one desired.
3. Management identifies detailed action plans to close the gaps.
4. Management engages in a structured implementation of those plans.[6]

Note that they are very similar to Champy's list but are not in the same order. For example, step 2 of Conner would be equivalent to steps 1 and 2 of Champy. Conner's step 1 (define the desired culture) is very similar to Champy's step 3 (articulate the values everyone must move toward). Since both approaches have been successful, it is not surprising they are similar. The primary difference is that Champy ends by saying we must start living the values that will define your culture. This implies that the culture (the way things are done) will now reflect the desired attributes of the changed culture. This is a very important, and necessary, final step. I believe Conner's sequence is more logical. For the purposes of this book, we will adopt that approach with one modification; we will add a fifth step to make sure institutionalization is addressed. The modified sequence will be:

1. Senior management defines the specific characteristics of the desired culture.
2. Management then conducts a "culture audit" to determine the gaps between the existing culture and the one desired.
3. Management identifies detailed action plans to close the gaps.
4. Management engages in a structured implementation of those plans.
5. Management ensures that the change is sustained so that the new culture is the desired culture.

Change that is Generally Consistent with our Culture (Minor Change)

When change is introduced in incremental steps, it is often difficult to recognize. Particularly those changes which are generally consistent with the existing culture? Clearly, if the proposed change is generally consistent with the existing culture, we will not be attempting to change the culture first. So how does this movement to the new desired culture happen? How does the culture tilt to the left toward the 20 degrees proposal depicted in Figure 7.2 happen? If the change is generally consistent with the existing culture, we consider it to be a minor change; if the change is radically different from the existing culture, we consider it a major change. The following comparison provides some of the answers to the question. How does this happen when the change is generally consistent with the existing culture?

Since almost every culture can accept the idea of cleaning up your shop, introducing 5S into your culture would be equivalent to introducing a change which is generally consistent with the current culture and be similar to the first arrow on the left of the figure, which is only about 20 degrees out of alignment with the culture. What then would it take to institutionalize this change? Well, apparently neatness in your shop areas was not the way your existing culture had done business, so the new culture would require that order and neatness become part of your culture. In our diagram in Figure 7.1, that would mean that the culture arrow would have to rotate to the left and align itself with the 20 degrees arrow representing the change. This is indicated in the Figure 7.2 below.

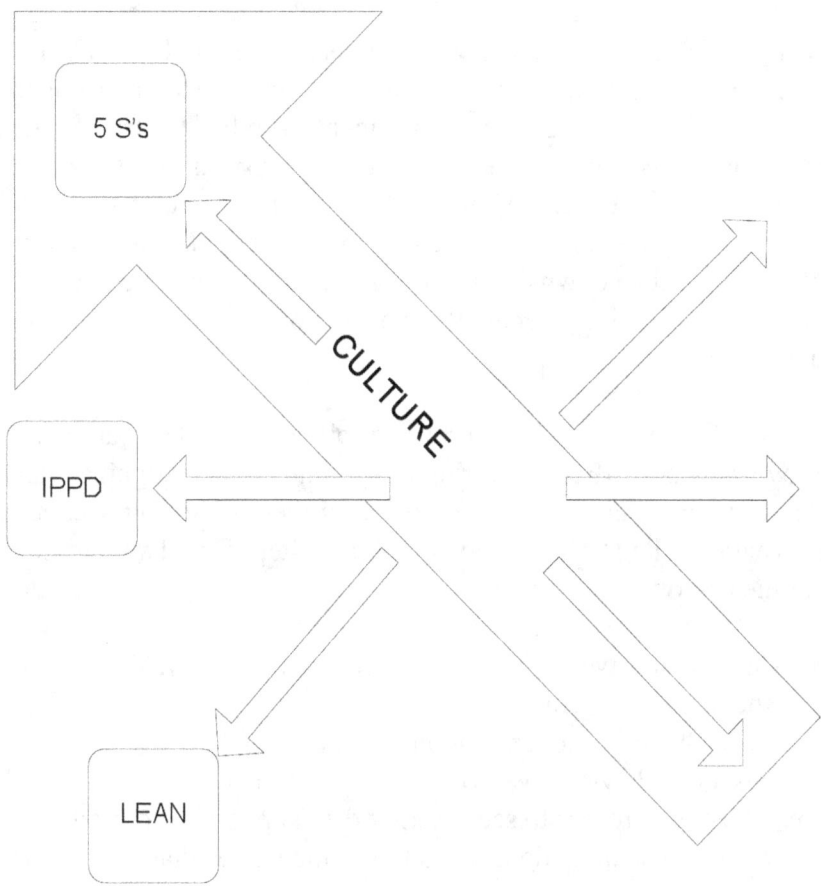

Figure 7.2 Alignment of Corporate Culture with Proposed Change

What would happen if you tried to go directly to LEAN manufacturing first? Well experience has shown that if LEAN is very different from what you are now doing, it would be extremely difficult and you may even fail. So in the case in which the proposed change is very much out of alignment (perhaps as much as 180 degrees) with the culture, what should you do? What this means is that before you introduce the change initiative, you have to change the culture first! This was first mentioned in Chapter 5 in describing the initiating phase. The most likely outcome is a failed change initiative.

Lets look at what can happen if you do not change the culture first. A good example of the failure to change the culture first can be seen in the wave of reengineering, which was undertaken by many companies, after the publishing in 1993 of the book, Reengineering the Corporation, by Hammer and Champy. It is estimated that, by 1994 70% of large companies in the United States and 75% of European firms undertook some form of reengineering initiative. While there were some notable successes, there were many more failures than successes and most of the reengineering changes did not last (were not institutionalized). This raised a lot of questions and this resulted in the authors revisiting the reengineering revolution to see what might have been left out. Clearly, they had covered most of the bases in the initiating phase, they had strong sponsorship, identified targets, and trained the agents through some of the principles of reengineering presented in the first book. However, one serious mistake was that no one seemed to address the question, "Who is affected and how by the reengineering initiative?" Because this question was not asked, Champy and Hammer misunderstood what a big impact radical change had on the management who had been asked to carry out the change and how much resistance was developed by existing cultures to radical change. While not as obvious, another question, "How are the benefits measured and captured?" also was not addressed with enough emphasis. Therefore, most companies did not see any benefits from their efforts, other than downsizing. Reengineering became closely linked with downsizing (without any productivity benefits), a conclusion that seems to haunt Champy and Hammer to this day. [3,4]

The result was that both Champy and Hammer wrote follow-up books to address these shortcomings. In Champy's new book, Reengineering Management, he recognized that management needed skills in how to change the culture to accept these radical new concepts. In his book he described what he called "The Five Not-So-Easy Steps for Changing the Culture." These steps are outlined below:

1. Find out the real values that drive the behavior of people every day. Very often they are not the ones in the published values statement.
2. Look for bad behavior that drives out the good.
3. Articulate the values and behaviors everyone must move toward.
4. Examine your management process to see whether they support or contradict the desired values and behaviors. [5] Start teaching, doing, and living the values that will define you culture.

Table 7.1 Changing the Culture (Major Change) versus Changes which are generally consistent with the existing culture (minor change)

MAJOR CHANGE	MINOR CHANGE
1. Senior management defines the specific characteristics of the desired culture.	This (step 1) is the desired benefit of the change project.
2. Management then conducts a "culture audit" to determine the gaps between the existing culture and the one desired.	This (step 2) comes from determining if this is a major change or not. In this case it is not, so the gap is small and closing the gap is highly likely.
3. Management identifies detailed action plans to close the gaps.	This (step 3) is the plan for implementation and includes such things as answering the question: Who is affected and how?
4. Management engages in a structured implementation of those plans.	This (steps 4 and 5) is the action taken by effective sponsorship of the project. For example, in the case of introducing 5S as the change, the sponsor must ensure the change is sustained until "being neat and orderly" becomes part of the culture. This is the most important step.
5. Management ensures that the change is sustained so that the new culture is the desired culture.	See above.

We had indicated earlier that if the initiating and implementing phases were done correctly, that it was very likely that the change would be institutionalized. We can see that many of the required steps for successful initiating and implementing maps nicely into the architectural culture change steps. Only the institutionalization phase is missing. This requires sustaining sponsorship, which must be continually done until it is no longer required. Again, using the 5S implementation as an example would mean that the sponsor and management must be continuously "walking the talk" about 5S by such means as formally and informally recognizing productivity improvements resulting as a result of 5S, by frequently checking 5S Communication Boards and 5S Routine Checklists, by recognizing the 5S levels of achievement, and by consistently commenting on the improved work environment created by 5S activities. These activities must continue even after the 5S techniques have been absorbed into the culture. Clearly, however, there will reach a point when these activities are no longer forced or require a great deal of energy from the sponsor and management. At that point, the entire organization will simply see 5S (a place for everything and everything in its place) as the "way we do business around here." That will be at the point when the change (5S) is institutionalized. When proper institutionalization takes place, it often goes un-noticed because it is now consider normal. This means you have successfully changed the organization!

Managing the Past, Present, and Future

When we successfully change the culture, it is usually because we have not only managed the change (future), but that we also have managed the past and the present. Just as initiating, implementing, and institutionalizing change is not a new management concept (we have just emphasized the need to complete the cycle), managing the past, present, and future, is not a new management concept. I was first introduced to this concept by the writings of Rosabeth Kanter, the author of Change Masters and other well known management books and papers. I have successfully used this concept in my work in industry. In fact, understanding the need to manage the past, present, and future resulted in an interesting personal story which I shall shortly relate; but, first let's discuss the general concept of managing the past, present, and future. [7,8]

Anyone who has had to undertake a major (or even minor) change while trying to keep the normal business activities on track understands the difficulty of multi-tasking while undergoing a major change of direction. It is difficult, to say the least, and it conjures up the rather vivid image resulting from such sayings as "It is difficult to remember we came to drain the swamp when we are up to our necks in alligators!" At least that is what we say in Louisiana!

When we speak of managing culture during change, we are essentially saying that we are using various methods to continually align the culture with the change strategy, or vice versa. This will become more obvious when we discuss Figures 7.3-7.6. If an organization's cultural environment is not managed well, people will feel that changes are coming at greater volume, momentum, and complexity than they can adequately assimilate. Some call this "Future Shock." others develop sayings to express this frustration of not believing they can handle all of the change being thrust upon the organization, such as the previously mentioned "up to our necks in alligators" as well as "the straw that breaks the camel's back." Managing a culture that is changing to a new vision is particularly difficult and means concurrently managing the past, present, and future.

Managers who are successful in managing the past, present, and future are usually aware of how much their organizations can assimilate at one time. Assimilation is the process we use to adjust to the implications of a major shift in our expectations. When management is successful in creating a climate in which change is viewed as normal, then change is our expectation and it is easier for us to assimilate new initiatives. Management can also improve the climate for change by providing as much information as possible on the change initiative and how it will affect the organization. When expectations match the reality of the situation, then organizations can more easily assimilate change. Providing truthful information is the best way to do this. When employees trust management, they are resilient and can assimilate large amounts of change. In understanding an organization's ability to assimilate change, Conner points out that there are really three levels of assimilation: (1) that required by micro changes which affect you, your spouse, and family, (2) that required by organizational changes that occur not just at work but within any institution (church, etc.) that affects your life, and (3) that required by macro changes that affect you as part of a large constituency (profession, race, etc.). While most focus on organizational changes, managers who are successful in managing the past, present, and future are generally aware of the impact on their employees of all three assimilation needs.[9]

Managing the Past

If culture is being changed to a new vision (future), this is often accompanied with the assumption that something was wrong in the past. This is not always true because it is often the environment in which the organization is in that has changed, and this results in the old methods no longer working. But even if something was wrong in the past, there are usually sufficient good happenings in the past which should be honored before we move on. Without this positive link to the past, particularly in organizations which have a history of success, it is often more difficult to be successful in the future. Hence, we need to find a way to honor the successes of the past, particularly when the workers undertaking the new initiative are strongly connected to that past. They must understand that frequently what they did before was good but the environment has now changed sufficiently so that the old methods which made them successful are no longer applicable. When the organization understands this, they will be ready to move on, particularly if you give them a brief time to mourn the losses. While this time should be very brief, they should be given some period in which it is OK to express grief for what is now no more. It is important to allow this time because those most associated with the past will be the likely targets of the change in the new initiative.

In managing the past, it is important to remember that most successful organizations were built on the shoulders of those who went before us. Acknowledging this before moving toward a new direction is important. For example, the military, particularly units like the United States Marine Corps, has a tradition of success that goes back to the beginning of our country. So while the weapons and tactics may change dramatically, the Marines continue to be successful by reminding every new generation of Marines of the many acts of heroism that preceded them. These are the qualities which must be remembered and which have allowed the Marines to continue to succeed despite the rapidly changing battlefield environment.

Companies that are successful in transition also honor their past (rather than just starting with a clean sheet as if everything that preceded did not matter). For example, when Carlos Ghosn of Renault took over Nissan after their merger, he addressed the question of how do you transform a company without destroying its identity. His answer was that you have to respect the dignity of the people even as you challenge them to overturn deep-seated traditions. By respecting them, you are respecting their past efforts and they are much more likely to be open to the changes being thrust upon them. Respecting them honors the past while moving on to better things. Ghosn said, " Inside Nissan, people recognized that we weren't trying to take the company over but rather were attempting to restore it to its former glory. We had the trust of employees for a simple reason, we had shown them respect. Although we were making many profound changes in the way Nissan carried out its business, we were always careful to protect Nissan's identity and its dignity as a company." By recognizing its former glory, Ghosn was honoring the past while moving the company to a new and better position.[10]

Perhaps another example of an actual case respecting the past and allowing employees to mourn the losses will be useful. This comes from my personal experience and it was obvious to me the value of mourning the losses. During the last years of my career in the electric utility business I became part of a newly formed strategic business unit, it was called the Generation & Transmission Strategic Business Unit (G&T SBU). It was formed as a result of a reorganization from autonomous operating companies into a central organization which would run the operations for all four companies. Another opportunity to morn the losses! The reorganization was designed to give us both economy of scale for operations and to reduce the number of persons required to run the organization effectively. The G&T SBU was formed from people and parts from the operating companies and required a great deal of energy and teamwork to make the new SBU operate well. However, we did it! We even took pride in our new organization. But less than two years after the formation of G&T, it was decided to separate the generation and transmission functions. This time it was a result of a changing regulatory environment. Deregulation was coming to the electric utility industry and it appeared that the generation side would be the first to be deregulated while there was continuing debate as to whether or not the transmission side would ever be deregulated. So while it made sense to separate the functions, it really took the wind out of the sails of the G&T organization.

During this period we were also undergoing a major quality initiative (yes, I have been there too!). During one of our Quality Action Team (QAT) discussions, we were talking about how difficult this change was going to be. Our expectations did not quite match the reality of the deregulation movement. During that discussion someone, I believe it was an executive secretary, suggested that we have a jazz funeral for the ampersand (&) since that was the only part that was going away, and it symbolized our G&T organization. We all thought this was an excellent way to get closure on the issue and move on.

Since some of you may not be familiar with New Orleans jazz funerals, a brief description is necessary. Basically a jazz band is hired and the leader of the band carries a picture of the deceased as they march in front of the casket to the burial site. The procession to the site is somber, as is the music. Once the eulogy has been given and the deceased is put to rest, the band strikes up festive music and a party and celebration ensue and everyone gets on with their lives. Getting the corporation to sanction this event was no small task, since at that time electric utility companies were still rather conservative, to say the least! However, we received permission and with the usual energy and initiative of the soon to be deceased G&T group, we found a casket, a procession leader (complete with tails and top-hat), wrote a eulogy, and in a couple of weeks had the event. The eulogy played a large part in the success of the event; it covered our pride in the G&T organization, our frustration at its early end, and our willingness to go on, all with a great deal of humor. The event was a huge success and became part of the stories we told to new employees as we moved on to the new organizations. One of the advantages of a jazz funeral was that it was brief and had the dual objective of honoring the past as well as moving on. And we did move on, knowing that our past efforts in G&T were recognized and were part of the change cycle process, which we began to expect would never end. We were transitionrd to the new organization with renewed energy and commitment. Since we did that in 1992, I have heard of other organizations, which have done something similar (and they were not even located in New Orleans).

Managing the Present

This is the difficult transition phase first discussed when we defined change. Change consists of moving through a transition phase (present) from the status quo (past) to a desired state (future). The transition phase is filled with uncertainty and long hours. Management's role during this phase is to reduce anxiety. This is, of course, no small task. The organization is going through change while still having to get the regular work done. And when the change is over, the organization will be forever different. So how do you reduce anxiety under these circumstances? By being truthful about what is happening and where the organization hopes to go. Since this is also the implementation phase, we can reduce anxiety by taking all of those steps that make for a successful and less stressful implementation. Such as determining who is affected and how. Then providing those who need training or additional help so that they will believe they have the capabilities to meet the challenges they are facing. Remember, when the organization believes that their capabilities will allow them to meet the challenges they face, then they will not be anxious and will be able to assimilate the change. Managing the present means that management is acting as the change agent for the change initiative.

Managing the Future

We talked about management's role in managing the past and present. The role in managing the future is really a leadership role, which is to provide a vision. This is what leadership does; it continually provides new direction to keep an organization viable. It must do more than provide the vision; it must live the vision. In other words, the leadership of the organization must walk the talk. Hence while the organization is struggling to handle the present (including the change initiative), the leader must continually remind the organization of the final goal and must provide visible and constant evidence of the importance of the goal. For example, in the case of the 5S, he must constantly reward conduct that supports the five Ss; sorting, simplifying, systematic cleaning, standardizing, and sustaining while letting the organization know that this is just the first step in becoming a LEAN organization (the vision). Once these ways (LEAN) become normal operating procedures, then the organization can move on to the next change cycle.

Change That Is Not Generally Consistent with Our Culture (Major Change)

Recall that we earlier said that if the change were major, that is, it is not consistent with the existing culture, then the culture would have to change before the major initiative could be successfully undertaken. We used some of the reengineering history as an example in our previous discussion.

What this really means is that if you have determined the change is major, you must change the culture before you begin to initiate and implement. Once you have changed the culture, you can begin the change cycle process described in this book. So, it should be perfectly clear that before you begin the change cycle you must know the difference between a major and a minor change. Remember the definition of major and minor change is organization specific! What might be a major change for your organization may only be a minor change for others. Major change does not have to do with the size, complexity, or cost of the proposed initiative; it has to do with how different the initiative is from the current way you do things. That is why the culture arrow diagram (Figure 7.1) is so useful when trying to understand the impact of change on your organization. To undertake a major change should be a business imperative, or as Conner says, it should be a "burning platform". [11]

So let's assume that you have correctly identified the need for a major change and lets also assume it is a LEAN initiative for your manufacturing process. How do you change the culture to get the right corporate environment to accept the major change? Well we already have the blueprint, the modified architectural approach to cultural change, but how do we actually carry it out?

To begin with, major change is just what it implies and it cannot happen overnight. Most major initiatives such as Total Quality, LEAN, Six Sigma, reengineering and similar undertakings, all take considerable time. In fact, they will take years. I am most familiar with Total Quality initiatives and the one with which I was directly involved in industry was laid out as a five-year plan. Even with a five-year plan, you have to decide what should be in the plan. Should it include milestones with the appropriate celebrations when they are reached? Should it include subsets of the initiative (for example 5S in the case of a LEAN initiative)? Should the culture change be part of the plan, concurrent with the plan, or preceding the plan?

My belief is that you must first change the culture before the change initiative begins because you have determined that the initiative is significantly out of alignment with the current culture. Hence, changing the culture first is really a preliminary step in initiating the change, and this step is driven by the major change. Thus, changing the culture and initiating, implementing, and institutionalizing the change as part of a continuum with many backward and forward links and often concurrent activities. In addition, I do favor pilot projects as milestones in the overall plan, particularly those that are subsets and supportive of the major initiative. This usually helps the organization become prepared for the major change and also allows for some early wins. For example, the 5S process is a subset of LEAN and, as we saw earlier, successfully implementing and institutionalizing it means that " a place for everything and everything in its place" becomes part of the new culture for the pilot program and a feature of the desired final culture.

How you approach major change is definitely organization specific and each of you need to decide for yourself whether it will be done as some of the earlier reengineering initiatives (radical change which required a clean sheet of paper) or gradual milestones that, over time, lead to a successful major change. Or perhaps some combination of these two approaches. One of the reasons that I have left the detailed discussion of introducing major change for this chapter is that much of the information developed up to this point, such as assimilation capability, capabilities versus challenges, and other change concepts, will be useful in helping you decide how you should address the initiative once you have determined it is major. To help in this process, let's walk through some of the milestones we might want to address if we were introducing LEAN manufacturing into a culture that is quite different from the characteristics of LEAN. We will use the modified architectural approach.

Senior management defines the specific characteristics of the desired culture: Here we would clearly want to develop our new culture in light of the attributes of LEAN such as the ability to accomplish setup and queue reduction; to improve process flow (including reducing variability); and to successfully implement 5S, Kaizen, value stream mapping, and others attributes associated with LEAN. While these are attributes of LEAN, do they really describe the desired culture? Not really, since reducing variability is an outcome, not a characteristic of the culture. So what should the characteristics of the culture be? Does it need to be trusting and open? Will that allow for a successful implementation? Is that sufficient? Is that different from the past environment? How do we determine what type of new culture we need?

Arriving at the vision of the desired culture is extremely important. Visiting companies, possibly in non-competing industries, that have accomplished what you want may be useful. During the visits, inquire about their culture rather than just their techniques of implementation. Is it an open and trusting environment? How important is that to the LEAN implementation? What is their reward system like? Is that important to their LEAN initiative? Remember the culture is defined by our beliefs and behaviors. What will be the required behaviors and beliefs in the LEAN environment? The question, " What do we want the culture to be?" should be asked in an iterative fashion with continual questions such as " If this becomes our behaviors and beliefs will that be the environment we need to embrace LEAN and make it succeed?" Sometimes the use of an outside consultant can help in defining and refining the vision of the desired culture. While you are determining the desired culture, you can often concurrently be addressing the next step.

Management then conducts a "culture audit" to determine the gaps between the existing culture and the desired one: We mentioned above that using a consultant to assist in defining the desired culture may be useful. When conducting a culture audit an outside consultant is essential, because of the difficulty of "knowing thyself." If we have a history of success, it is difficult for us to determine that there is something about the existing culture that needs changing. If we do the cultural audit ourselves, we run the risk of not getting a true picture of our current culture. We may wind up with what we say we are rather than what our actions indicate we are. Outsiders are better equipped to ask questions such as, "What do you like about your current culture and what would you like to see change?"; whereas management is more likely to become defensive while asking such questions. When management does the culture audit, the end result may be a less than accurate culture audit. Outside consultants who specialize in culture audits also know the right questions to ask and how to interpret them. Get some help in doing your culture audit.

Management identifies detailed action plans to close the gaps and then engages in a structured implementation of those plans: In completing this step we can avail ourselves of all the tools which were developed in the initiating and implementing phases. This is another reason to wait until this chapter to address major initiatives that require changing the culture before the change initiative, such as LEAN, is introduced. All of the change concepts, such as who is the sponsor and who is affected and how, are all applicable to changing the culture. In fact, they may be of even more importance since changing a corporate culture is usually one of the most difficult changes to make. To improve your chance for success, you need to determine if the company and its employees can assimilate the culture change or do they need more training and perhaps even reassignment of personnel to be successful. The concept of managing the past, present, and future is particularly important when you are changing the culture. Recall that much of the reengineering efforts failed because they failed to honor the past. Ghosn succeeded when he lead the cultural change and restructuring at Nissan because he respected the past. Once you have developed the plan, then you must put it into action.

Management ensures that the change is sustained so that the new culture is the desired culture: During this phase the sponsorship must be sustained with strong focus on the desired state (new culture). This has to do with managing the future while you are working through the change in the present. The desired state must always be the goal and the milestones to that goal must be celebrated when they are achieved. Actions and outcomes that support the attainment of the ultimate goal (vision of the new culture) must be recognized, encouraged, and rewarded, while behavior that supports the old status quo must be eliminated. Consider the Olympic athlete whose goal is to compete (and win) in the Olympics. To reach that goal he/she must constantly train to reach peak performance to compete against world class athletes. In reaching for that goal (competing in the Olympics) his/her training becomes a way of life. Not only does the athlete talk about being in the Olympics, he/she " walks the talk" by his/her behaviors and beliefs. Then the reward may be an Olympic medal. This is what management must do; it must focus on the new culture and behave in such a way so that it can be achieved. When this is done, it becomes the way we do things; the desired culture becomes our culture.

Moving from Minor Change to Major Change in Steps

Another question we need to ask is: " If we determine the initiative is going to be a major change should you change the culture first and then directly introduce the major change or should the major change be undertaken as a series of related steps?" To illustrate this concept we will use Total Quality Management (TQM) as an example. Total Quality Management would certainly be considered by most as a major change. Major change also takes time and most agree major change should be done with long term plans usually no less than five years.

In many companies this would require changing the culture first. But some would advocate that TQM can be best done in a series of planned intermediate steps in which small adjustments to align the culture are made in each step. This is an alternative to changing the culture first (often also in a series of planned steps), and then introducing the major change in one step. Clearly, there are strong similarities to each approach. Changing the culture prior to introducing the major change will also generally require a series of steps which introduce the desired culture change. This is not unlike introducing the major change initiative in a series of steps in which the culture must be changed incrementally in each step. Since the two approaches are so similar, an example illustrating the difference between the two is appropriate.

Perhaps the best example of the two methods is the different approaches of two well known gurus of the quality movement, Deming and Juran. Probably no individual has had more influence on quality management than Dr. W. Edwards Deming. The Deming philosophy focuses on bringing about improvements in products and service quality by reducing uncertainty and variability. However, Deming generally did not lay out improvement "programs". Rather his goal was to change entire perspectives in management, and often radically. His approach was akin to the reengineering approach of starting with a "clean sheet." Consultants who follow the Deming approach often spend a great deal of time interviewing top management and, if unconvinced that top management will change before introducing the quality concepts, they often refuse to take on the change initiative.

J. M. Juran proposed a simple definition of quality: "fitness for use," which essentially means that quality is related to product performance that results in customer satisfaction and freedom from product deficiencies. Juran's approach to management was quite different from Deming's. Juran did not propose major cultural change in the organization. Instead, he sought to improve quality by working within the system's existing culture. This is similar to the results of the 1992 International Quality Study which suggested that quality improvement programs were most successful when introduced in a manner that is most closely aligned with existing practices. [12]

Let us examine the introduction of a major change, in this case TQM, in a series of steps. In practice, the steps would likely be four or five distinct steps. However, for the purposes of this illustration we will consider only three steps. That not only simplifies the example but it also allows us to use what I like to call the hierarchy of quality (1) culture, (2) programs, and (3) tools. These categories are closely aligned with the concept of the foundation needed to support quality principles as expressed by Evans and others. [13] That foundation consists of three parts, (1) an integrated organizational infrastructure, (2) a set of management practices, and (3) tools and techniques. These two sets of three almost mapped directly into each other, as shown below:

CULTURE	←	→	INFRASTRUCTURE
PROGRAMS	←	→	PRACTICES
TOOLS	←	→	TOOLS & TECHNIQUES

Clearly, in the hierarchy of quality it is easier to introduce new tools than it is to introduce new programs, and it is easier to introduce new programs than it is new cultures. For example, suppose we wish to introduce TQM in three steps starting with the introduction of the tool, the PDCA cycle. PDCA is a tool for introducing continuous improvement by going through the steps of Plan, Do, Check, and Act. The steps form a never-ending cycle and can be applied successfully to a range of problems from simple to complex. Hence, the idea would be to introduce the organization to the PDCA method of improving quality through continuous improvement. Training could begin on simple problems and as the organization becomes more proficient with the tool, it could then be applied to more complex tasks. Once the organization begins to regularly use PDCA to improve quality, it has become part of the organization culture and a more sophisticated type of continuous improvement, such as Kaizan, can be introduced.

Kaizan is a Japanese word that means gradual and orderly improvement. Kaizan is a broad based continuous improvement philosophy which looks for improvement in all areas of business. Once the concept of continuous improvement has been introduced and accepted through the PDCA tool, the organization becomes ready to apply continuous improvement to all areas of business. Once Kaizan becomes part of the culture then the organization is ready to move to the next level, that of TQM.

TQM represents the complete change to a quality culture by integrating quality principles into all of the organization's management systems. Once this becomes the way the organization does business, then the transformation to a quality culture is complete. This may take several years and, as stated before, may require more than just three steps. To illustrate the changes that take place we have mapped the three steps (PDCA, Kaizan, and TQM) onto the culture map, as shown in Figures 7.3 through 7.6.

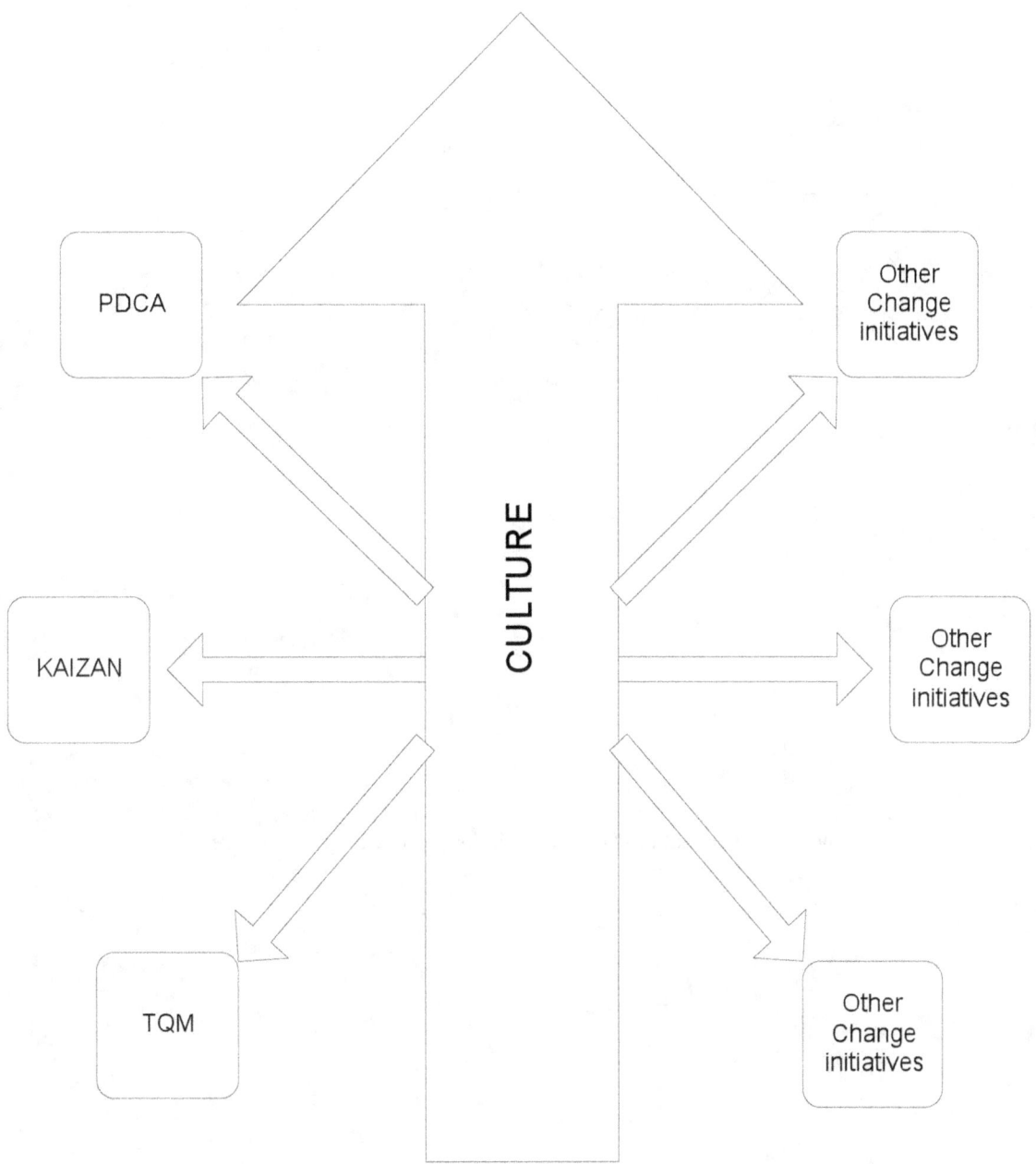

Figure 7.3 Initial Relationship of Culture to PDCA, KAIZAN, and TQM

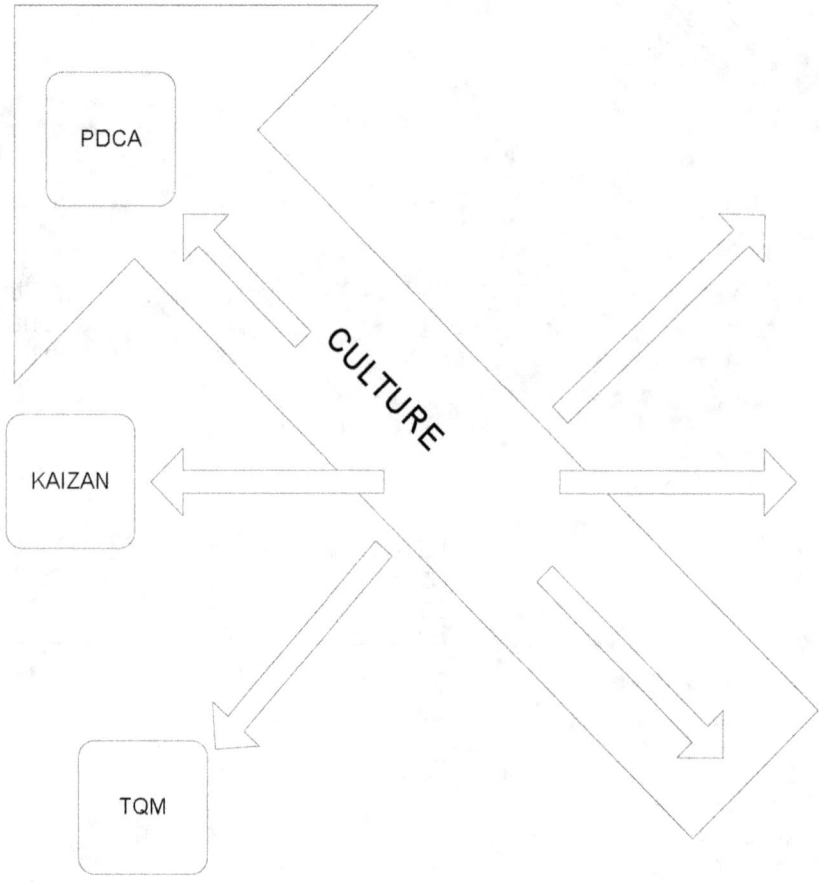

Figure 7.4 Alignment of PDCA methodology with Company Culture

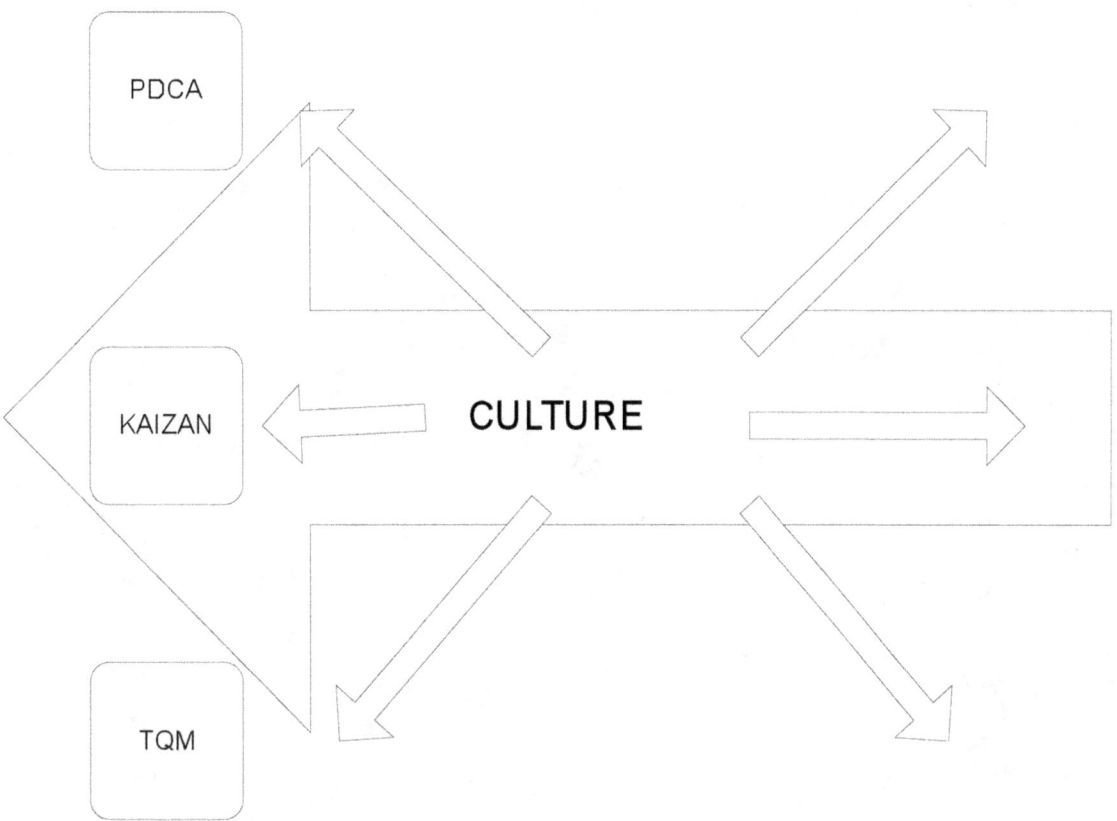

Figure 7.5 Alignment of KAIZAN program with Company Culture

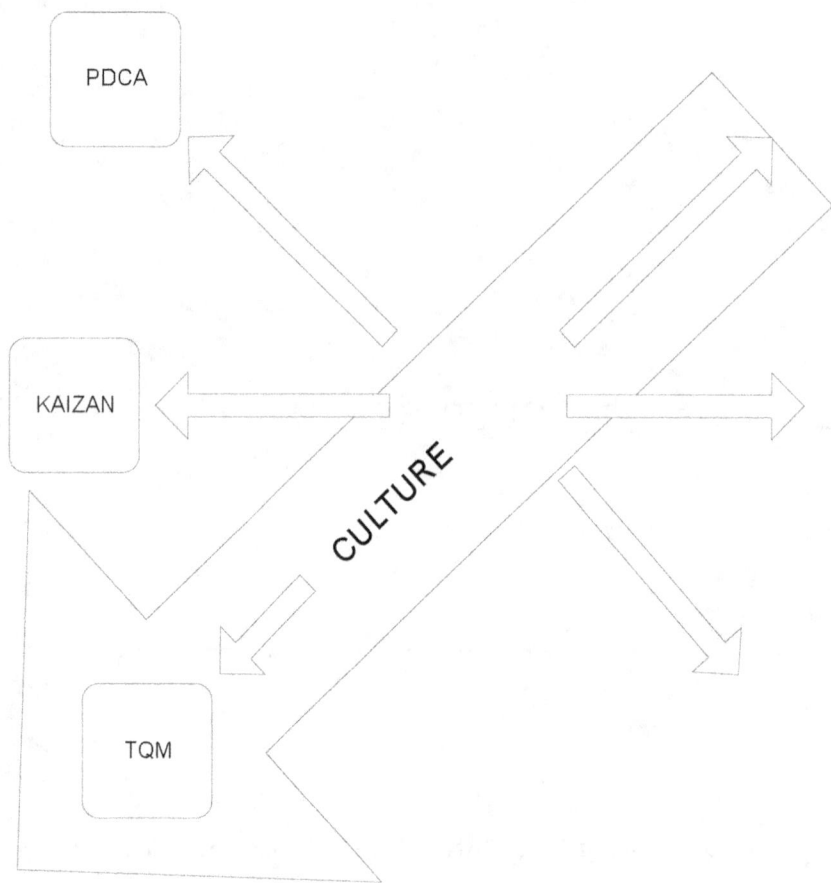

Figure 7.6 Alignment of TQM culture and Company Culture

Note that in each step, the organization should not proceed to the next step until the new change has been absorbed into the organization. That is, until the culture becomes aligned with the change initiative. By changing the culture in steps, it is less traumatic for the organization and it gives milestones at which time the organization can assess whether or not the new initiative (such as the PDCA cycle) has become part of the culture. If not, the organization needs to take additional action to ensure that the change becomes the way things are done before going to the next step. This must occur at each step. Recall that it was indicated earlier that the transition from the present culture to the final desired state (in this case, a TQM culture) may take more than three steps, but the process would be the same, it would simply have more incremental steps involved in changing the culture.

We have stressed the importance of getting the culture to realign with the change in each step before moving to the next step. Essentially, this means we have changed the culture in incremental steps. We have already seen how the modified architectural approach to changing the culture is applied to a major change. It would seem that these principles would also apply to incremental cultural changes and, of course, they do. A comparison of the architectural change steps to the changes happening in the incremental step approach is shown in Table 7.1 for the step in which the change required is to move from PDCA to Kaizan.

Table 7.1 Comparison of Major Change with Incremental Change

MAJOR CHANGE	STEP CHANGE (cultural change before going to Kaizan step)
1. Senior management defines the specific characteristics of the desired culture.	1. Senior management determines that the PDCA cycle tool is needed to initiate continuous improvement in the organization.
2. Management then conducts a "culture audit" to determine the gaps between the existing culture and the one desired.	2. Management identifies those areas in greatest need of the PDCA tool.
3. Management identifies detailed action plans to close the gaps.	3. Management develops a plan for the roll out of the use of the PDCA tool, including training and selection of groups to first implement tool.
4. Management engages in a structured implementation of those plans.	4. Management begins the roll out to initial units and ensures that the successes of the early adopters are recognized and that all units utilize the new tool.
5. Management ensures that the change is sustained so that the new culture is the desired culture.	5. Management continually reinforces the fact that PDCA is the method (tool) of choice in achieving continuous improvement until it becomes the way the organization operates without any needed encouragement. Now the organization can move to the next step (Kaizan).

In summary, we can say that the change is institutionalized when the new way (the change) becomes our way of doing things. When this happens it becomes our culture. The change and the culture are now aligned. Remember, if the change is major, then the culture will have to be changed first. An alternative to changing the culture before beginning the change initiative is to change the culture in planned steps with the initial steps being those that are already most closely aligned with the existing culture. Culture change should be linked to the change initiative. During the change process you must manage the past, present, and future. When the future and the present merge, the change is complete; the change has been institutionalized.

In my view, developing the major change initiative into logical phases or milestones and then introducing them in incremental steps is the best approach. The incremental steps should begin with those most closely aligned with the existing culture and then move in a series of steps to those milestones which are most unlike the existing culture. This was illustrated in Figures 7.3 through 7.6. For this approach to be most successful it should be recognized that the company culture must be changed at each step (i.e., must be aligned with the incremental change) before proceeding to the next step. Once you have gone through all of the steps, the existing culture will have be changed to the desired culture and you will have institutionalized the change.

Suggested Exercises

1. Have a group discussion on why institutionalization, that is becoming the way we do things, is the most difficult phase of the change cycle. Discuss what can be done to improve the institutionalization phase.

2. Define, in your own words, how you would know when a change is institutionalized.

3. Discuss some desired changes which could fit most easily (minor change) into your current organization. Do you think they could be institutionalized, why?

4. If you were the CEO, how would you describe the desired new culture (step 1 in the architectural approach to changing the culture)? Why?

5. Is changing the culture before a major change the same as introducing the major change in increments, why?

Notes

1. Scott, Suzanne and Einstien, Walter; Strategic Performance Appraisal in Team-Based Organizations: One Size Does Not Fit All, IEEE Management Review, Volume 29, Number 4, Fourth Quarter 2001.
2. Henley, Gene, Two Shipyards Realize Immediate ROI from Five S, National Shipbuilding Research Program (NSRP), The Navigator, Winter 2001.
3. Hammer, M. & Champy, J. (1993) Re-engineering the Corporation New York: Harpers, 1993

4. Pink, Daniel, Who Has the Next Big Idea?, Fast Company, September, 2001.

5. Champy, J. ,Reengineering Management, HarperBusiness, 1995.

6. Conner, Daryl, Managing at the Speed of Change, Villard Books, 1993.

7. Kanter, Rosabeth, Change Masters: Innovation and Entrepreneurship in the American Corporation,

8. Kanter, Rosabeth, When Giants Learn to Dance, Simon & Schuster Inc. , 1989.

9. Conner, Daryl, Managing at the Speed of Change, Villard Books, 1993.

10. Ghosn, Carlos, Saving the Business Without Losing the Company, Harvard Business Review, January, 2002.

11. Conner, Daryl, Managing at the Speed of Change, Villard Books, 1993

12. Evans, James and Lindsay, William, The Management and Control of Quality, Fifth Edition, South-Western/ Thompson Learning, 2002.

13. Evans, James and Lindsay, William, The Management and Control of Quality, Fifth Edition, South-Western/ Thompson Learning, 2002.

Chapter 8

CHANGE MANAGEMENT WORKSHEETS

*The questions which one asks oneself begin, at last, to illuminate
the world, and become one's key to the experience of others.*
James Baldwin

If we can develop a series of questions to be answered prior to beginning each phase, based on the successful change management concepts of others, we will greatly improve our own chances for success. Hence, in this chapter we have taken the concepts of the last three chapters and developed them into a series of questions for each phase to be addressed prior to the beginning of each phase. This is an important pre-planning step. Pre-planning is an important first step in almost any process. Planning helps to insure quality and consistency.

In the Quality movement, most major quality tools and procedures always began with planning. The well known, Plan, Do, Check, Act (PDCA) continuous improvement cycle advocated by Shewart and Deming begin with the all important first step of planning. Joseph Juran, another major player in the development of total quality management, developed what he called the Quality Trilogy: (1) quality planning, (2) quality control, and (3) quality improvement. At the time he proposed it, few companies were engaged in any significant planning or improvement activities. He, too, recognized the importance of planning.[1] Proper preparation and planning is also essential in change management. Prior to each phase of the change cycle, proper planning for that phase should be accomplished. Worksheets have been developed to help you to do that.

The Worksheets are designed to assist the change management practitioner in successfully initiating, implementing, and institutionalizing change. They incorporate the principles we have introduced in previous chapters into a series of questions and checks which will insure that no important planning point is missing. These worksheets are not project management tools, in the normal sense; they focus on the human element in change rather than the process. They require you *to consider the people involved* in the proposed change as well as the culture in which the change is to occur.

The Initiating Worksheet

The format of the worksheet will be introduced, then each question or step will be accompanied at the end of the worksheet with an explanation as to how that question should be addressed. Shown next is the first worksheet, The Initiating Worksheet, it can generally be fit on one page but may require attachments to provide complete answers.
Note: The company identified in the Worksheet is the company which is changing, that is they are the sponsoring or funding agent. Many proposals are written in response from a

Request For Proposal (RFP) from a funding agents and in almost every case the responders to the RFP who submit proposals come from companies other than the funding agency. In these cases, it is important to note that the core values, roles people play (sponsor, agent, target), business case, etc. all refer to the funding organization which requested the proposal and do not refer to the organization responding to the proposal. If the proposal for the change initiative is internal then there should be no confusion since everyone is in the same organization.

INITIATING WORKSHEET

Provide the requested information for the proposed project and answer the questions below.

1. What is the business case for this proposal?

2 .Is this proposal aligned with your company Core Values?

3. What are the company procedures required to get the proposal approved?

4. Who is involved in the project? Who is their supervisor? Are the organizations involved directly or indirectly connected (develop a Project Organizational Relationship Chart *on a separate piece of paper*- this is an <u>important step</u>).

5. Who is the target?

6. Who is the agent?

7. Who is (should be) the sponsor? Does this require cascading sponsorship?

8. Who are the decisions makers? Are there persons *not in the decision chain* who can influence the decision (Called Influential Advocates – they can sometimes veto proposals by their informal power)?

9. Does this proposal represent a major change? Give justification for your conclusion.

10. Can this project be developed in increments that are more closely aligned with the existing culture? If yes, what would be the steps (increments)?

11. What analysis tools should you use to justify the proposal? Do they include a method for capturing the benefits? What measures will be used to determine if the change is successful?

12. What is the language (hot buttons) of the decision makers? Can you use this effectively in the proposal?

13. Are there any things in the next two phases (implement, institutionalize) that may come up in the approval process?

Let us take a close look at the questions posed on this worksheet and discuss why they are important in preparation for the initiating phase of change and how you should approach addressing them.

What is the business case for this proposal? This clearly should be the first question asked when undertaking change. Does this proposal make sense to the company's core business? Is it intended to improve profits or is it required to meet a competitor's capability? If there is no business case, this project should be dropped. No one should change simply because everyone else is doing it; it must be important to the business. If it is major change, it must be a business imperative.

Is this proposal aligned with the company Core Values? This is an interesting question because it assumes you know the company core values. For some, this question should be preceded by another question, what are the company core values? Why is this question important? Because it is easier to make change when it is aligned with company core values; pointing this out, will make the change more acceptable for many. For example, if one of the company core values is that they value training as a competitive edge, then if this is part of the proposal, that training should be emphasized. Often a proposal seems to be quite different from what we have been doing. Perhaps it involves going into a new market or introducing some new state-of-the-art equipment. These may be things the company has never attempted but when the employees are reminded that extensive training will accompany the new initiative and "that is how we always do things" then most will recognize that although they are going in a new direction they are doing it in a manner that is familiar to everyone. One of the reasons people resist change is because they do not want to give up their comfort zone, if you can convince them that they are taking something of the old way of doing things (a core value) with the new proposal, it gives them an anchor upon which to build the new initiative. It takes away some of the discomfort of the perceived change. Including a well know core value in the new initiative is a way of taking something from the old comfort zone into the what is hoped to be the *new* comfort zone.

What are the company procedures required to get the proposal approved? This sounds simple, but make sure you fully understand the requirements to get a proposal approved. Generally each company has some formal or informal procedure for getting new proposals approved. Sometimes it is a formal annual budget meeting requiring extensive cost/benefit analysis, sometimes it is a simple one or two step process. The point is, do not get your proposal delayed or disapproved because you did not include all of the normal company requirements. Even if this is an internal proposal, it will help if you assume that this was a proposal to an outside agency that came in the form of a Request for Proposal (RFP). Often good proposals are thrown out in the first round of elimination because all of the requirements stated in the RFP were not addressed. Make sure you have met all the company requirements.

Who is involved in the project? Who is their supervisor? Are the organizations involved directly or indirectly connected (develop a Project Organizational Relationship Chart on a separate piece of paper- this is an <u>important step</u>). This is the first major step in reviewing who needs to be involved in this project. Without this step, we sometimes forget groups or individuals who will be affected until we are prepared to implement. By leaving some important players out of the loop, you subject the proposal to additional resistance during the implementation phase. The way a Project Organizational Relationship Chart is developed is as follows:

1. First identify the persons who should be involved in this project. They often fall into the categories of direct role, indirect role, or informational role.

2. Next identify the supervisors of those persons identified in the previous paragraph. This is important because often persons involved in new projects are not all from the same group or division and you will have to get the supervisor's support or at least his/her concurrence to work on the initiative.

3. Now having identified the participants and their supervisors, visualize overlaying a company organization chart on the participants. This will identify relationships which will have to be dealt with in order to reduce resistance and make the project successful. This chart is also extremely helpful in confirming who should be the target, agent, and sponsor.

Who is the target? The Project Organizational Relationship Chart will help to properly identify the target, the target is the person or groups who will have to change. The target is the first person(s) to be identified. It should be noted that if the sponsor is not already on board with the proposal, which is often the case when a major change takes everyone out of the comfort zone, then *the sponsor may have to be treated as a target as well as the sponsor in the initiate phase.* This is because you have to change the position of the sponsor to get approval to move to the next phase in which the " ultimate target" of the proposal then becomes the focal point of the change.

Who is the agent? Again the Project Organizational Relationship Chart will assist in properly identifying the agent(s). The agent is the person who must make the change happen. The agent should be the second person identified. If the proposal is made in respond to an RFP, the agent is often a person from the outside organization making the proposal. In that case, there is often a primary contact from the funding organization who is assigned to the change agent's team.

Who is the sponsor? Here is where the Project Organizational Relationship Chart is really helpful. By now we will know whether the target and agent are in the same group/division. We also be able to see whether we are dealing with line, triangle, or square relationships of the sponsor/agent/target. This will tell us whether or not we have to go up additional levels to get the appropriate sponsor in order to make the project successful. If we have to go up several levels to get the appropriate sponsor, then this will require cascading sponsorship in which we must make sure that each sponsor in the chain of command from the primary sponsor to the target is on board.

Who are the decisions makers? Are there persons not in the decision chain who can influence the decision (Called Influential Advocates – they can sometimes veto proposals by their informal power)? One of the decision makers should obviously be the sponsor. Remember the sponsor is a person who can legitimize the change. That means he usually has the budget and other resources to make it happen. While the sponsor is not always a member of the budget committee, their knowledge that he is committed to the project (including a willingness to spend his portion of the company budget on it) will go a long way in getting approval. There are, however others, who can influence the decision and they are often overlooked to the peril of the proposers. These are the Influential Advocates, those who have the primary decision maker's confidence. This typical happens in areas such as information technology, in which primary decision makers rarely make a move without the concurrence of their chief information officer. If he/she is not on board the project will probably not be supported so you need to treat them the same as a primary decision maker. In a change management class in which new initiatives were reviewed, one of the things the students had to do was to identify influential advocates. Several of the companies were small family owned businesses and in most of those cases the influential advocate was identified as the wife of the owner. Make sure you know who these influential advocates are, and treat them like primary decision makers.

Does this proposal represent a major change? Give justification for your conclusion. This is really a question about the culture of the company. One of the best tests for determining whether or not it will be considered major, is how different is it from the way the company presently does things (how different is it from our culture). Other tests are when capabilities exceed the challenge, when reality is very different from company expectations, and when it is perceived by the *target* as major change. Why is this important; because if it is major it will require a lot more planning and resources to get the proposal through the three phases of change?

Can this project be developed in increments that are more closely aligned with the existing culture? If yes, what would be the steps (increments)? This is related to the previous question. If it is major, it may make more sense to break the change down into steps, beginning with the one that most closely aligns with the current culture (even if it is a small beginning step for a big project – this gives you a chance for an early win which may reduce resistance to the remaining part of the project). There is a danger in doing it in increments if only the first step will be funded the first year and that is that the remaining, and generally most important, steps may not be funded. That is why the initial proposal should contain all of the steps with costs and time schedules and approval should be sought for the entire project, not just the first year. It is not always easy to get this type of approval but an effort must be made to discuss the whole project and the effects of not completing each step. On multi-year projects, each year when the project is brought back to the budget process, progress on the steps that are completed should be included in the budget presentation.

What analysis tools should you use to justify the proposal? Do they include a method for capturing the benefits? What measures will be used to determine if the change is successful? The analysis tools are generally those associated with the company procedures required to get approval. However most company cost/benefit calculations do not require a measurement section in which measures are developed which will be able to tell if the project is a success. This is extremely important to change management projects in which we want to institutionalize the change. If actual measures can be provided, the chances that this initiative will be institutionalized (will become the way we do things) is greatly enhanced. Being able to prove the value of the project will insure that the sponsors make this new approach a part of their standard competitive company tools.

What is the language (hot buttons) of the decision makers? Can you use this effectively in the proposal? By hot buttons we mean things that are not only important to the company but are important to the company right now. For example, if reducing cycle time is a major corporate direction, then if the project proposed can reduce cycle time, incorporating that as a major benefit of the proposal will enhance its ability to get it approved and will also tend to continue to get support for it throughout the implementation and institutionalization phases. The hot button can be something that is even considered negative, for example "downsizing" or reducing headcount through attrition. If you can show that the proposal will improve efficiencies to the point that the task can be done with less people, then again, this will enhance your chances of approval.

Are there any things in the next two phases (implement, institutionalize) that may come up in the approval process? All of the phases are interconnected, although if you do not get past the approval stage you do not have to worry about the next two phases. The purpose of this question is to take a little time to look ahead and to use the next two worksheets to think about possible stumbling blocks or critical questions. For example, the VP of IT may be at the budget meeting and ask how will this affect your IT resources. The initiate worksheet deals primarily with *who* is affected (involved in the project) and not *how* they are affected. By looking ahead at the implement worksheet you might view it with the knowledge of who will be at the budget meeting (approval meeting) and recognize that some groups will be very much affected and you might want to at least let them know what you are planning. Being able to say you have been discussing this with the IT group and they feel comfortable with the proposal but will give a detailed support statement once the project is improved could keep the proposal discussion moving, while having no answer could be a show stopper. You might also be asked "Do you think this will be accepted by *whoever is the target group?*" You can refer to the change management techniques you intend to apply, particularly the meetings and monitoring in the institutionalizing phase. This is not a question that you need to spend much time on but you should at least read over the worksheet for the next two phases before going to the budget meeting.

Answering these questions on the Worksheet will greatly enhance the planning effort for the new initiative and will improve the chances for successful implementation. This, of course, brings us to the second phase of the change cycle, the implementation phase.

The Implementing Worksheet

Shown next is the second worksheet, the Implementing Worksheet. It generally consists of two sheets but may require additional sheets to complete the questions.

IMPLEMENTATION WORKSHEET

Reflect upon the people who will be involved in the approved project that now has to be implemented. In the implementation phase it important to determine who is affected and how? This will help to identify resistance to the proposal. Provide the requested information and answer the questions below:

1. How will you keep the sponsor informed and involved in this project?

2. Who will be on the project team? How will they be organized?

3. Understanding and Reducing Resistance (This is provided to assist you in completing item 4.)

What's In It For Me? This is an equity question that is generally asked by everyone affected by the change. To determine how well a change may be received you have to determine both the positive outcomes and inputs and well as the negative outcomes and inputs. If the net is positive the change will generally be accepted. If the net is negative the change will be resisted. Here are some examples of positive and negative inputs and outcomes to assist you in analyzing those affected by your project.

possible increases in outcomes	increase in inputs
More pleasant work environment, Less tension, more job satisfaction, More opportunities for advancement, Better service to customers, Salary increase, grade increase, or higher-level title, Reduced dependence on others.	More work in entering data, More tension, Bringing higher level skills to the job, Effort in learning a new system, Assignment of additional tasks, Need to spend more time.
possible decreases in outcomes	decrease in inputs
Reduced job satisfaction, Reduced power, Threat of loss of employment, Reduced importance, control, Increased monitoring and accountability.	Ease of usage, Less effort, Reduced manual effort, Less rework due to fewer errors.

4. Who is affected and how?
To insure that no one is left out of your analysis use the following groups. In the space provided indicate who (group or individual) is affected. Also include how they are affected (see item 3 for help).

Project Management Group (Agent – See Initiate Worksheet)

Who	How

Direct Users Group (Target – See Initiate Worksheet)

Who	How

Indirect Users Group; those who benefit from project (Sponsor – See Initiate Worksheet)

Who	How

Infrastructure Group ,those that provide support, training, hiring, etc. (Advocates – See Initiate Worksheet)

Who	How

5. Has the development of these "Who is affected and how" groups resulted in additional needs such as training, communications, or other actions necessary to ensure the successful implementation of the project? Will these actions alleviate some of the negative effects discussed in item 3? If so, write down these new concerns/requirements below:

6. How will you capture the Benefits? This should be in dollars. If you can not capture the benefits the change may not be institutionalized.

7. How will the team and other participants be rewarded for a successful implementation? Will these be monetary or some other form of recognition? Will the team share in the captured benefits? Are the rewards consistent with core values and supportive of the new desired behavior?

A close look at this Worksheet clearly shows that change management deals primarily with people and the culture of the organization. This Worksheet, as you might expect, becomes an extension of the previous worksheet. In the first worksheet we determined who was involved in the change and what role they played. What was not accomplished then,, was to determine how these people involved in the change are affected. How they are affected will frequently determine whether or not they will resist the change and how vigorously they will resist. So now we need to determine "who is affected and how?". But before we do that we need to make sure we keep that all important person, the sponsor involved.

How will you keep the sponsor informed and involved in the project? Once the sponsor has helped to get the project approved and has agreed to provide the resources, his job is far from over. If we have picked the sponsor correctly, he has authority over everyone involved in the project and hence has the authority to keep the project on track should it run into unexpected resistance. So how do we keep him informed? The best way is to have formal milestone reviews of the project which are presented directly to him. In this way, he can intervene and take corrective action, when necessary. It has been shown that the frequency of milestone meetings has a direct correlation to the success of change management projects. It is also important that he be keep appraised of the project in informal ways other than the project milestone review. Depending on the circumstances you may want to make sure this project gets on his agenda for other meetings as well as discussing the project when informal opportunities arise. A good change agent is always planning on how to act when those opportunities arise. The point is, most sponsors have many duties and projects which require their attention so the change agent has to plan to keep him both informed and involved during the implementation phase. He will be needed when resistance is identified.

Who will be on the project team? How will they be organized? During the proposal stage (initiate phase) very few assignments are made, often not even the project team leader is finalized. This is because not all proposals will be approved so it is premature to assign persons (other than being identified as potential resources) until the project is approved. Once the project is approved, however, the project team must be quickly assembled. This may be the first time the sponsor is needed because most likely the team members will come from various groups and often those group leaders do not want to lose their valuable people for extended periods of time. Hence, you may have to get the sponsor to intervene with the supervisors of the persons you need for the project implementation team. The organization will most likely be a matrix organization so it is important that the roles of the team members be clearly defined by the team leader along with responsibilities and accountabilities of the members (boundaries for the team). If you want to succeed you will want to assemble the best team possible. Since there is usually a tension among competing persons for these resources, it is important that you maintain sponsor support.

Understanding and Reducing Resistance. While everyone likes to be involved in a challenging assignment there can be downsides to this type of assignment. Hence, participants will generally ask the question " What is in it for me?" This becomes an equity issue so the worksheet provides tasks and events which can be perceived as requiring more or less work with greater or lesser satisfaction in order to help you decide whether or not the participant is more or less likely to resist the change. If the persons on your team do not report to you, a rule of thumb is that if your effort requires more than 10% of their normal work effort, they may be ineffective unless you make special arrangements with their direct supervisor.

Who is affected and how? Since the Project Organizational Relationship Chart has already identified who is affected by the change, the real task here is to determine how the person is affected. To do this the procedure suggested by Fisher and Wesolkowski is highly recommended.

The organization is broken into four groups, the project management group, the direct user group, the indirect user group, and the infrastructure group. Using these four groups should result in covering everyone in the organization that might be involved in any way.

Project Manager Group: This is the implementation team that has been put together for this project. These are the change agents. How they might be affected will depend on the circumstances surrounding their assignment to the team. Under the "who" heading each team member should be listed by <u>name</u>. Using the actual names is important because each individual may react differently. For example a very proficient professional may wind up getting assigned to several teams and sees this additional assignment as taking away from his ability to go a good job on his other projects, so he may resent this assignment rather than being pleased. In the "how" category, consideration, using the equity guidelines, should be given as to how each person may be affected by this assignment. Another example could be that it is well known that a certain team member, while the best available, is apprehensive about this assignment because he knows his functional boss is unhappy about his absence from his normal duties. This means the team leader will have to expend additional energy to make sure both remain satisfied during the life of the project.

Direct User Group: The direct user group is the target group, these are the people who will probably have to change the most. How much they have to change will probably affect how much resistance they will have to the change. In many cases their work may be easier. You need to do a careful equity analysis of the target group because they are the focal point of the project.

Indirect User Group: This can be best considered those who benefit from the changes required in the direct user group. It could be someone down the manufacturer chain from the direct user or it could be the sponsors who are clearly expecting this change to improve the organization, hence they would be benefactors of the change. Indirect users can also create negative consequences as well as benefits. For example, the person down the line from the direct user may have to speed up his work because of the improvements by the direct user. Hence it is important to do an equity analysis on anyone affected by the changes by the direct user, including those in support functions in the organizational infrastructure.

Infrastructure Group: In the previous section we mentioned that support groups can be affected by the actions and needs of the direct users. When initiating new projects one of the most overlooked groups are the support groups. Since they are not directly involved, they are often left out of the planning and funding until the implementation plan requires them to react to something. One of the most often missed requirements is the need for additional trainers. Many initiatives require that employees acquire new skills, skills which are often taught by the training section or human resources department. The proposal may also require changes in such departments as accounting and legal. Hiring practices may also be affected by the proposed change. Considering who will be affected and how for the infrastructure group requires carefully analysis so that no affected group is overlooked.

Has the development of these "Who is affected and how" groups resulted in additional needs such as training, communications, or other actions necessary to ensure the successful implementation of the project? Will these actions alleviate some of the negative effects discussed in item 3? If so, write down these new concerns/requirements below: Answering this question correctly will often identify some requirement that has been left out. It will often give evidence of potential resistance and the project leader must develop a plan to counter this resistance.

How will you capture the Benefits? This should be in dollars. If you can not capture the benefits the change may not be institutionalized. This is an important an often forgotten step. While surprising as it may seem, benefits (including monetary) promised during the proposal (initiating phase) are rarely followed up by management to see if these predicted benefits have been achieved, much less captured. The implementation plan should have some method of capturing the benefits. Real savings or increased revenue will always catch the attention of management and will improve the chances that this newly implemented initiative will become a permanent procedure (institutionalized).

How will the team and other participants be rewarded for a successful implementation? Will these be monetary or some other form of recognition? Will the team share in the captured benefits? Are the rewards consistent with core values and supportive of the new desired behavior? Some initiatives require changed behaviors from the past (change the culture). During the implementation phase is the best opportunity to develop rewards for the success of the initiative. If a behavior is being changed, those who exhibit the new desired behavior should be rewarded. The rewards can be personal recognition or monetary awards. For example, if the new procedure requires a new team effort, then team rewards should be developed such as gain sharing or other means of rewarding the entire team for its success. If there is no reward system for the changed behavior, it will be difficult to sustain the successes of the initiative and it may not become institutionalized.

The Institutionalizing Worksheet

The last worksheet is the Institutionalizing Worksheet. It is generally provided as a three page document, and again, completing it may require additional sheets.

INSTITUTIONALIZATION WORKSHEET)

The institutionalization phase is the reinforcement and consolidation phase. In this final phase you must insure that the change initiative becomes part of the culture. Unless the culture changes to include the new change as part "of the way we do things" then the change does not last. Remember, if the culture and the proposed change are not aligned, culture always wins. While the Sponsor is important in every phase, his importance in the institutionalization phase may be the most important. Without his strong continuing support the initiative may slip back into its old form before its gets institutionalized.

Once the change has been initiated, management and the organization must engage in constantly teaching, doing, and living the values of the new change. In other words, management and the organization must constantly "walk the talk" associated with the new change. If the change is going to be sustainable, it must become the way the organization does things (institutionalized). The change agents play a major role in this phase by mentoring and assisting the sponsors and targets to live and do the new way.

In this final stage it is especially important that the *sponsor rewards actions supporting the new initiative and continually extols the benefits captured during the pilot program and the follow on* activities. He should also remind everyone of the original business case and why it is still a business imperative that this initiative become institutionalized.

Activities required for the Change Agents

Pre-Institutionalization Planning Activities

Several things must be completed, or near completion prior to the beginning of the institutionalization effort for the change initiative. These activities must be driven by the change agents designated in the initiate phase. During this final phase, the change agents should be very active. Assisting presenters in incorporating the important points mentioned above into their formal and informal communications. While communications should be adjusted for specific audiences, all presenters should begin their meetings with a mention of the change initiative. This discussion should always begin with the theme based on the original business case. This concept of beginning each meeting with a topic related to the new initiative comes from the Total Quality Movement. By placing this as the first topic, the organization sends a reinforcing message that this initiative is important and needs to become permanent. Typical topics for discussion would come from the pre-planning list shown below. For example, at a foreman's meeting it could be about the appraisal system or the reward program, at a department head's meeting it could be about the benefits of the initiative to achieve corporate goals or about how it links to and supports other important activities

1. The first and most important activity is to get back with the primary sponsor to insure he/she understands the importance of why he/she must stay engaged in order to make this initiative a part of the "way we do things". One way to do this is to request a formal meeting to present the following items.

   a. Provide concrete evidence (early wins, benefits captured, etc., collected during the implementation phase) to the sponsor(s) on the importance of the initiative.
   b. Formally link this initiative with core values and all appropriate existing initiatives and norms (culture) of the organization. This will help to show how and why it is important to integrate the new initiative into the way we do things.
   c. Reinforce the business case with an easily identifiable "theme" of the new initiative. You must be able to state the reason this change is important to the organization and why it should be permanently adopted. This should be done in a few sentences that are clear and understandable to everyone.
   d. Encourage the sponsor to make the goals of the initiative part of the personal appraisal

system. What gets done is what gets measured! This should be done at each level and should be integrated directly to each person (group) work load. This step will go a long way in institutionalizing the new initiative. If necessary, reduce pre-initiative work loads (even if it is temporary – this shows the importance of the new initiative) by eliminating non-value added tasks to allow time for the new change initiative

e. Encourage the sponsor to develop a reward system that recognizes those behaviors which support the new initiative. Often with out an aligned reward system, the new initiative will slowly revert back to the old ways. This, like including the initiative goals as part of the appraisal system, will go a long way to institutionalizing the initiative.

2. One the sponsor has agreed on the need for the activities mentioned above, the agent will assist the sponsor in developing specific topics and meeting dates with the impacted groups. These discussions and meetings must continue until the initiative is institutionalized.

<u>Communication with the Executive/Management Group (Cascading Sponsorship)</u>

1. Conduct executive awareness training: Once the sponsor is on board, awareness of the new initiative must first be spread among key employees (the cascading sponsors). Executives have many things on their plates, however, they need to have information on the importance of this initiative if they are going to back it and they need to know that the Primary Sponsor backs the program.

a. Awareness training should include the points made above, and whenever possible the Primary Sponsor should make the presentations. These presentations should focus on how this initiative is assisting in meeting corporate goals and how it supports corporate core values. Typical opportunities for presenting this talk are shown below:

CEO Meetings

Departmental (Vice Presidents) Meetings

Special Events (Recognition Ceremonies, Training Seminars, etc.)

b. The change agent should develop a plan to have the Sponsor speak at these events that are scheduled during the first 18 months of the institutionalization phase. The change agent should keep notes on the group to whom the talk was presented along with the points that were emphasized, along with comments from the target group. It is important that this schedule is maintained in order to keep the importance of the initiative in front of the key employees.

<u>Communication with the workforce (targets)</u>

1. The change agents need to assist the key employees (cascading sponsorship) to mentor and train their managers and supervisors to carry the message to the entire workforce.

a. These communication channels should be both formal and informal, listed below are some typical opportunities to communicate in most companies.

Special Events (Recognition Ceremonies, Training Activities, etc.)
Superintendent Meetings
Supervisor Meetings
Foreman Meetings
Appraisal Reviews

b. The change agent should assist as many managers and supervisors in getting the word out on the new initiative. He should meet with as many managers and supervisors as possible and keep notes on whether or not the initiative was mentioned, at which meeting, which points about the new initiative which were emphasized, along with comments from the managers/supervisors on how well the new initiative is being accepted. This should be done for the first 18 months of the institutionalization phase.

Company Specific Meetings

The change agents should work with each group (sponsors and targets) to determine which meetings are scheduled or occur on a normal basis that can be used to emphasize the importance of the new initiative. The change agent should keep an accurate record of all meetings which introduce or discuss the new initiative. He should develop a specific list and follow up on the actions taken at these meetings. He needs to attempt to measure the acceptance of the new initiative so he will have some feeling as to when the new initiative becomes part of the culture.

It will be helpful to develop a list of both sponsor and target meetings that can be candidates for emphasizing the importance of the new initiative.

Your company specific recommended list of meetings:

This important worksheet does not consist of questions to be answered, rather it gives lists of activities that must occur during this final period. In this case the agent must directly assist the sponsor in developing his messages and this becomes a primary output of this phase. In addition, the agent must insure that the activities and messages developed in this phase actually happen (sponsor must walk the talk.) The relationship between the agent and the sponsor is important because he must convince the sponsor, who already has a great deal on his plate including other implementation initiatives that need his attention, to continue expending energy and time to institutionalize an already successful implementation. This tradeoff is probably why many good initiatives with successful implementations never get institutionalized.

The change agent should track all meetings that mention the new initiative for the first year. At the end of the first year of institutionalization an assessment must be made as to whether or not the change initiative has become part of the culture. If not, the process should be continued until it becomes the way we do things. How will you know when it is institutionalized? When it continues to get done without the need for constant reinforcement program developed in the institutionalization phase

Chapter 9

CASE STUDIES AND YOUR COMPANY

"Who has self-confidence will lead the rest."
Horace

The previous chapters were aimed at showing that change is both inevitable and manageable. Viewing change as normal means that you will be assimilate change without fear and anxiety. Confidence comes from knowing that your capabilities can meet the challenge of change. The tools (the worksheets) developed in the previous chapters were provided to give you confidence that you could initiate, implement, and institutionalize change. The question is, "Are you ready to lead change?"

Knowing methods and being self confident in using the methods are two very different things. We become confident when we continually apply the methods with good results. As we older folks like to point out that experience does actually count! However remember that Deming also liked to point out that experience alone was not sufficient, you had to understand the cause and effect of the events you are experiencing in order to apply them to future events. Of course, it is also possible to gain this experience vicariously by getting others who have actually applied the methods to share their experience with you. A good way of gaining confidence in new methods is to apply them to your own past experiences, both good and bad, and see if the methods would have worked or would have shown why a past experience was bad. Applying the methods (worksheets) to past projects will provide confidence to try the worksheets on new projects.

This is precisely what I do when introducing some of these techniques and tools as part of a class I teach on managing technology. Two of the written assignments have to do with applying these techniques to a past project (I also give the option to use it on an existing or future real project) and make comments and observations as to the validity of the processes. The two assignments are: (1) a project which the student initiated or advocated (or would like to) or a new initiative and (2) a project which the student implemented or would like to (a new project). These assignments were all individual efforts but we did discuss them in class to build up the confidence of the students that these tools and techniques actually work. This sharing of experiences helps to build confidence in the methods. I encourage you to not only try the methods but share them with others and encourage them to challenge and comment on the results.

I also give them an example in which I do the same, that it, I apply the techniques to a past successful project of my own and see if the success factors we have developed actually make sense to them in actual cases. The case I picked to analyze and share with the class had to do with a project I led when I was still doing real engineering work in the electric utility industry. I will share that experience here to show how to benchmark these methods against past experience. As you will see it is not necessary to follow every step of the worksheet to realize that this approach works.

The specific project had to do with the efforts to uprate our high voltage substations in the early 1980s. While we both initiated and implemented this successful project (we became the first utility in the United States to design and operate an uprated substation), I will only cover the initiation phase. More will be said about what uprating means later but lets first look at the steps we outlined in Chapter 5 on initiating or advocating change projects. If you recall, the steps for successful advocating were:

1. Define the objectives of the proposal
2. Describe the methodology to accomplish the objectives
3. Understand how the corporate culture will affect the change
4. Determine if the proposal represents major change
5. Determine which parts of the organization will be required to support the change (this will help to determine who the sponsor, agent, and target will be)
6. Follow company procedures and use the appropriate analysis tools for advocating (cost/benefit, etc.)
7. Determine who the decision makers are
8. Use the language of the decision makers

We will benchmark each of these success factors against the high voltage substation uprating project, but first let me provide a little bit of background of the project itself.

The Louisiana Power & Light Company Example

In 1983 Louisiana Power & Light Company (LP&L) became the first Electric Utility to successfully uprate a 115 KV Substation to 230 KV operation without changing the insulation level in the 115 KV electric substation. The importance of this is that, simply put, more power can be transmitted at higher voltage levels than at lower levels. Uprating refers to those methods which allow you to successful operate at the higher levels with minimal change to the existing system. Since this was the first in the country you might think this was a major change for our company, yet it was not, as we shall see in a moment. It also brought us both praise (for our pioneering and innovative work) and criticisms (from those who thought we were taking an unnecessary risk). Lets check the steps one at a time. Much of the electrical engineering concepts will not be covered in detail since the point of the exercise is to determine the efficacy of the change method and not the engineering concepts. Those interested in the engineering details can refer to the reference in the notes at the end of the chapter.[1]

Define the objectives of the proposal and describe the methodology to accomplish the
 objectives :This relates to the following steps of knowing the culture, whether it is major change, etc. The impact on those following steps will depend on the objectives and methodology. In this case, the objective was to produce a more robust electrical system at minimal additional

cost. The most difficult technical question was how could the uprate be accomplished without changing the insulation level. This break through came for our experience with SF6 Compact 500 KV substation design which, in essence allowed us to use judicially placed arrestors to keep the same insulation level.

Understand how the corporate culture will affect the change : At that time (early 1980s) LP&L was very much open to innovation and change. They pioneered automation in generation plants (one of their early control units is in the Smithsonian Institute) and the use of helicopters in transmission line construction. More importantly, they had planned, through strategic purchases of dual rated equipments and other design consideration to uprate the system from 115 KV to 230 KV.

Determine if the proposal represents major change: Considering the preplanning to uprate, this was not a major change even though its success would make us an industry leader. LP&L had energized 115 KV substations at 230 KV as early as the late '60s to study potential conversion problems. They had also developed a policy of purchasing dual-rated transformers (115x230) in anticipation of the change. The proposed change was aligned with the culture of the company.

Determine which parts of the organization will be required to support the change (this will help to determine who the sponsor, agent, and target will be) : The primary group involved would be the substation design group (my group), the system planning group would also be required to provide the appropriate studies to show the need for the uprate and the division substation crews and installation engineers would be required to do the actual field modifications. All were involved in the planning and all ultimately reported to the Chief Engineer, a very likely choice for the sponsor and, in fact, the actual sponsor.

Follow company procedures and use the appropriate analysis tools for advocating (cost/benefit, etc.) : At that time there was a great deal of emphasis on doing more with less. If uprating could be proven as both feasible (it still was untried) and cost-effective, then there was high probability it would be funded in the budget meetings. Transient analysis was used to locate arrestors to limit over-voltages, one of the primary concerns. The Chief Engineer, who was the key technical person at the budget meetings, was well acquainted with this type of analysis. In addition, we were familiar with the company's standard cost/benefit requirements and included that analysis in the proposal.

Determine who the decision makers are and use the language of the decision makers: At that time the Chief Engineer was the key decision maker in determining the allocation of the budget for funding projects. Because he was part of the previous history of preparing for the uprating, uprating was already part of the language of the decision makers.

Get a Sponsor: As previously mentioned the Chief Engineer was the sponsor and a very effective one, when it came to uprating, he "walked the talk" and everyone knew he was behind the project.

The project was approved and in 1983 at the LP&L Pontchartrain Substation the first uprated substation was successfully energized. It is still in service. Several other uprated substations followed and LP&L assumed the role of industry leader in uprated substations.[1]

When we did this project, we were unaware of the steps outlined in Chapter 5 although we were aware of some of the principles associated with them. It can be easily seen that most of the required success factors for advocation were in place at the time the project was first proposed. The second example is provided from Rick McGregor, a former Shell Oil employee who has been a guest lecturer in my course. During the course he covers a technique developed by Shell called the Technical Limit Drilling (TLD) process, which enabled Shell to dramatically improve their deep water drilling capabilities. Rick McGregor benchmarked that success against the methods we developed for initiating major projects. The Shell Oil example follows.

The Shell Oil Company Example

Define the objectives of the proposal and describe the methodology to accomplish the objectives : The initiative was driven by a need to make Shell's drilling cost programs competitive within the U.S. oil and gas industry, and to make economically viable a substantial portion of Shell's exploration portfolio, which was not achieving economic benchmarks due to high well costs. In 1999, Shell Offshore, Inc. (a subsidiary of the parent company, Royal Dutch Shell) brought the first application of the TLD process to the U.S. and to the deepwater Gulf of Mexico.[2,3]

Understand how the corporate culture will affect the change: Shell's cultural transformation had begun in the early 1990's, fueled by a decline in corporate financial performance and loss of competitive position. The old corporate culture of organizational bureaucracy and functional silos was being replaced by a culture that emphasized teamwork focused on business results. So the corporate environment was open to new teams and new ideas. The TLD process application was the idea of an ad hoc team formed to review options to reduce drilling costs on one particularly challenging exploratory well. Once the opportunity was aired to management, sponsorship of the team was quickly taken up by a senior manager. One of the reasons for the rapid acceptance and support by management was the recognition that this particular process had potential far beyond the one well application.

Determine if the proposal represents a major change: In retrospect, this probably did not represent a major change although it did require some adjustments. Shell already had in place many of the elements to propagate this "new" integrated process of project time and cost savings that is now called "Technical Limit Drilling." For the important elements of disciplined project management in planning and execution, Shell was already an industry leader. This strength was now married to a process in which knowledge sharing and real time application of lessons learned became critical to success. Other critical enablers such as resources and skilled staff also were not an impediment. Probably the biggest, and most important, hurdle was to create and sustain a "no blame" environment, which would encourage widespread involvement and commitment by all the participants. This part of the initiative probably did represent a significant change in our culture and while senior management was committed to the latter, it really could not employ it without some structured training. Outside experts were brought in to institute the training and to facilitate the initial pilot application.

Determine which parts of the organization will be required to support the change (this will help to determine who the sponsor, agent, and target will be): The drilling manager's buy-in to the process was critical for success. He became the team sponsor and provided unprecedented time and support for this particular effort. He was key in approving new resources and, because of his high level of monetary authority, changes were implemented at lightning speeds. Later, he was instrumental in establishing a center of excellence from which to propagate this process throughout the organization.

Follow company procedures and use the appropriate analysis tools for advocating (cost/benefit, etc.): It was a simple matter to develop a justification for the TLD process in the Gulf of Mexico after the similarities of the successful application in the offshore Thailand environment became clear. Comparing our proposal to those successful operations was important information to the decision makers. After learning all the key ingredients of the tool/application, and after applying a rudimentary value analysis, it was quite obvious what the potential benefits were. The challenge from senior management (and the project Sponsor) was how the initial pilot application might be accelerated. The support for this was strong and the staff resource commitment was obtained after only one asset managers meeting.

Determine who the decision makers are and use the language of the decision makers: As mentioned above, the decision maker's language was part of the approval procedures, that is, the use of value analysis and the listing of potential benefits. In addition, they always want to evaluate the risk and knowing that essentially this same method had been used successfully, by Woodside Offshore Petroleum in Thailand, was also what they wanted to hear.

Get a Sponsor: The drilling manager was an effective sponsor, both as an initiating and sustaining sponsor. This definitely was a major factor in the success of the project. The pilot project was completed in 1999, within about 9 months of the introduction of the TLD process. Results were so positive that the program was mandated for all future drilling wells in the U.S. offshore and continues today. [2,3]

In these examples, the success factors for initiating change were clearly present. This evidence gave Rick and me confidence in the methodology. For you to have confidence in these methods, you must apply them to some of your past experiences in attempting to implement change. You may wish to choose a failure to see if some of the critical factors we have presented are missing. We often learn more from our failures than from our successes.

The Northrop Grumman Ship Systems Example

While benchmarking the model against past projects will give a sense of confidence in the methodology, the best way to validate a model is to use it on a new project and observe its effectiveness. The author and some of his colleagues were funded by one of the University of New Orleans Centers of Excellence, The Gulf Coast Region Maritime Center (GCRMTC) to use the change cycle method to assist Northrop Grumman Ship Systems (NGSS) in institutionalizing a project on the cost of poor quality. The full report can be found in the Final Report for GCRMTC dated 3/30/05.[4] The previous examples compared the success factors of introducing change to past projects. This example and the last one (FEMA Example) will be more useful because they actually use the worksheets. In the NGSS example you will see actual examples of the completed worksheets.This is perhaps the best example of using the method with a large company because it illustrates how the worksheets were used, including the development of the project organization relationship chart and the "who is affected and how?" matrix. What follows is an overview of that project.

When this project began, the NGSS cost of poor quality (CoPQ) initiative was itself just beginning. This was a typical cost of poor quality program as seen in many companies but customized for the shipyard. One of the reasons NGSS was undertaking this approach was to provide a means of selecting the best projects for a major productivity improvement initiative that was already underway, Lean Six Sigma. It was also to provide both executives and shop foreman with accurate data on the cost of shipbuilding. Lean Six Sigma has been used in other industries and essentially is a synergistic approach using two methods, Lean, to reduce non-valued added tasks in the process, and Six Sigma, to reduce variation in the process.

As pointed out throughout this book, introducing a new initiative requires three distinct stages; initiating, implementing, and institutionalizing. In this example, this cost of poor quality program had already gone through the first two stages and our role was to provide methods and steps to enhance the institutionalization of the Cost of Poor Quality (CoPQ) program at NGSS. By institutionalize, we mean becoming part of the corporate culture of NGSS, becoming the way things are normally done.

The program had been initiated and implementation had begun, however it was being implemented in stages. Typically cost of poor quality initiatives have four components; internal costs, external costs, appraisal costs, and prevention costs. In the NGSS case, it was determined that the greatest opportunities for improvement were in the internal cost area, particularly in the rework area. The roll out of the first segment of CoPQ to the operation forces was in January, 2004. The initial version contained only labor rework (internal cost category). Later in April the capability to include the breakdown costs by defect code was added. Because of the newness of the program, it was necessary for the Principal Investigators to conduct interviews and team meetings to determine the present status and acceptance of the new CoPQ program. These meetings and interviews were also used to determine if some of the requirements of the initiate and implement phases had been met; that is, had sponsors, agents, and targets (adopters) been identified and had it been determined whether or not this was a major or minor change (adoption of cost of poor quality program). To facilitate this approach a project organizational relationship chart was developed. It is shown in Figure 9.1.

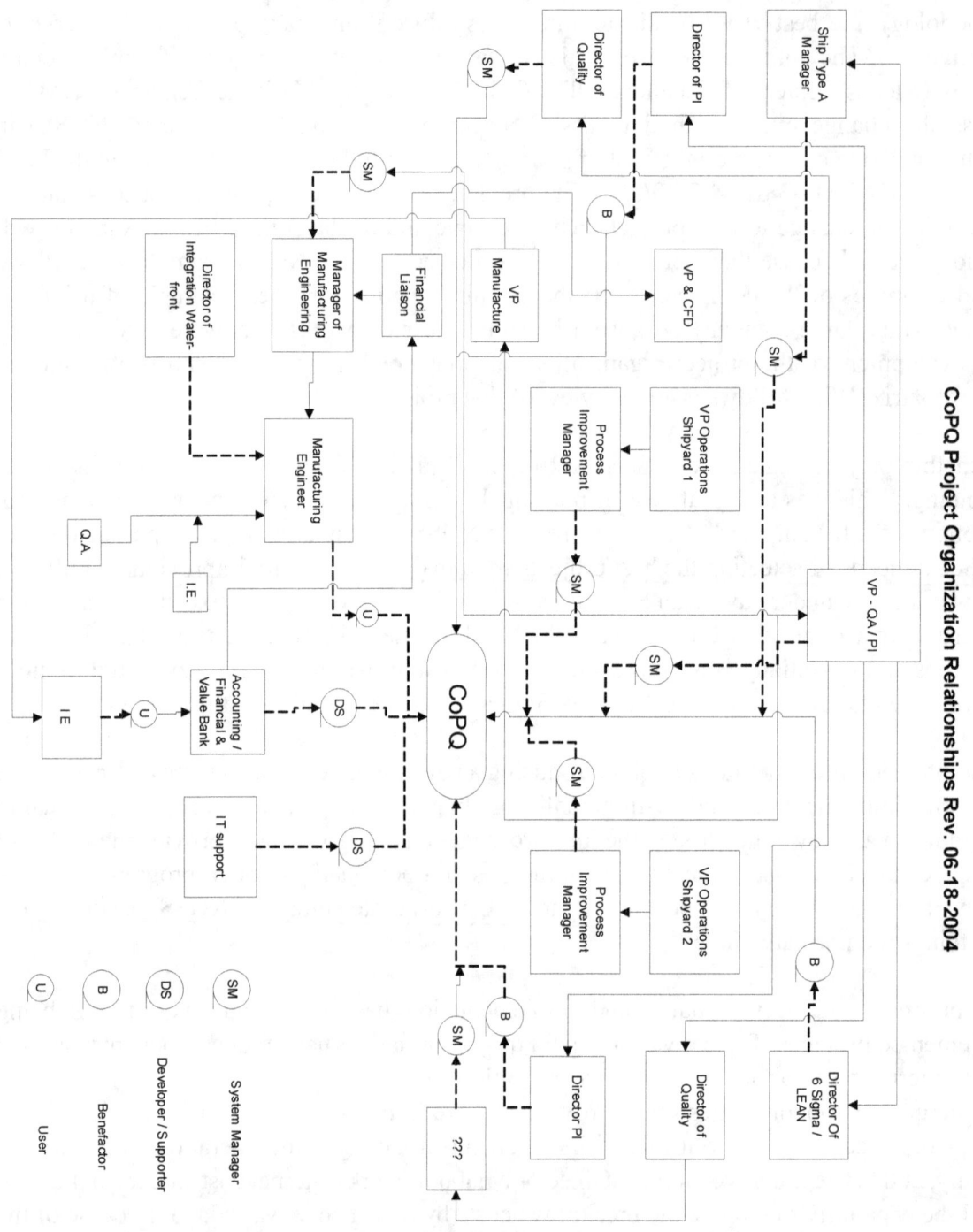

Figure 9.1.

This project organizational relationship chart was used primarily to determine those persons who were directly, or in some cases indirectly (support), involved in the CoPQ project. This essentially was determined to be the *agent* team. The agent team was essentially all of the persons reporting to the Vice President of Quality Assurance and Process Improvement (QA &PI) and are shown as system managers on the chart. This chart was used to verify who were *targets* which were identified as users on the chart. The primary users were the manufacturing engineers. There were *sponsors* indicated on this chart and they were primarily the line Vice Presidents such as the VPs of Operations. However to get all of the sponsors this chart had to be expanded into the larger organization chart with the President being designated as the *sponsor* and cascading sponsors being designated as the line Vice Presidents that reported to him. This chart also had some advocates such as the Vice President and Chief Financial Officer (VP & CFO).

Using this chart and the Implementation Worksheet for this initiative, NGSS verified our findings and conclusions on *sponsors, agents, and targets* so we could move to the final phase, the institutionalization phase.

The completed Implementation Worksheet as was done during the project is shown below, in most cases, the responses by NGSS are shown in *italics*:

IMPLEMENTATION WORKSHEET
FOR NGSS CoPQ PROJECT

Reflect upon your approved project that now has to be implemented. Provide the requested information and answer the questions below:

How will you keep the sponsor informed and involved in this project?

The agent(s) in Q&PI need to develop regular communications with the Operating groups in the Build, Integrate, and Deliver sectors on the amount of dollars accumulated through cost avoidance (and eventually cost savings) attributable to CoPQ/LEAN/Six Sigma. Q&PI needs to be the reporting agency to the President (Sponsor) on progress being made by CoPQ activities.

In the following groups indicated, who (group or individuals) are affected. Also include how they are affected.

Project Management Group

Who	How
1. *CoPQ Team Leader from Q&PI group*	1. *CoPQ TL must align the CoPQ program with the LEAN and Six Sigma initiatives. CoPQ should become the primary source of opportunities to use LEAN and Six Sigma for improvement. CoPQ TL must keep records of progress of CoPQ. Must make sure CoPQ supports Operating group goals and initiatives (alignment)*
2. *NGIT Support*	2. *Must provide IT support for existing program of labor rework and future additions to CoPQ (scrap, etc.)*
3. *"Validation Process Team"*	3. *This group provides the link to the Financial/Accounting group for validation of the results of CoPQ activities. Also will provide a process of charging time to CoPQ/LEAN/Six Sigma projects so that a realistic ROI can be calculated and used for justification for cost avoidance/cost savings. Group will develop as standard for calculating ROI for CoPQ/LEAN/Six Sigma projects.*

Direct Users Group

Who	How
1. Superintendents, Foreman, Craftsman, etc.	*1. Will use <u>the CoPQ software program</u> to convert labor rework jobs into cost of poor quality categories to populate the CoPQ data base. Eventually the CoPQ data base will include more than just labor rework (material, etc.).*
2. Manufacturing Engineers	*2. Will use <u>the CoPQ data base</u> program to assist indirect users to identify and prioritize high "profitability" opportunities so that the appropriate Six Sigma and LEAN projects/ tools can be applied. They will recommend solutions and calculate cost/benefit numbers to justify each project. Once the projects are approved and completed they will do an outcome assessment on the project to see if the calculated cost/benefit numbers were correct.*

Indirect Users Group (those who benefit from the actions of the direct users)

Who	How
1(Sr. VP Programs, VP Ops-Shipard #1, VP Ops-Shipyard #e, and VP Supply Chain Mgt.	*1.a. Will benefit from the CoPQ completed projects by improved productivity in the Build, Integrate, and Deliver phases of shipbuilding.* *1.b. Will use the project outcome assessments, in conjunction with the Finance/Accounting function to verify cost avoidance/saving. Once Finance/Accounting has validated the results they will use the validation results to verify cost savings and budget adjustments. If there are differences in the validation process from the method used by the manufacturing engineering in their cost benefit analysis, the manufacturing engineers will be required to align their methods with the Finance/Accounting validation methods. The ultimate goal is to have the cost/benefits and the validation methods the same.*

Infrastructure Group

Who	How
1. Human Resources	1. Provide the necessary resources (additional manufacturing engineers, training, etc.) to support the CoPQ initiative.
2. NGIT	2. Provide the necessary resources (IT personnel) to support the maintenance and modification of the CoPQ software.
3. Finance	3. Provide the necessary resources (personnel and training) to support the "Value Bank Process" team.

Has the development of these "Who is affected and how" groups resulted in additional needs such as training, communications, or other actions necessary to ensure the successful implementation of the project? If so, write down these new concerns/requirements below :*Training on the new system (CoPQ) is on going. Agents and operating persons (targets) will determine additional training on an as required basis.*

A look at the implementation worksheet will quickly demonstrate that three of the groups directly map into the previous definitions, that is, the Project Management Group is the same as the *agent* group and the Direct User Group is the same as the *target* group. We have to expand the definition of the Indirect User Group before it becomes clear to which group they relate. The Indirect User Group can be further defined as those who benefit from the work of the direct users, this would mean they are similar to the *Sponsor* group, although persons other than sponsors could be in this group. Before we examine the Infrastructure Group we have to be reminded that this expanded matrix considers "how" they are affected, not just who is affected. Thus in the infrastructure group we realize that such groups as HR will be affected if more Manufacturing Engineers need to be hired or more Black or Green Belts need to be trained. This will affect support departments in the infrastructure group such as IT and others and as that is further developed the comments on the last entry on the worksheet may need to be expanded.

Development of the Institutionalization Worksheet;

Comments are entered under the major categories on the worksheet. Below are the entries made for this particular initiative. These comments were a result of interviews and interactions with personnel in the shipyards to determine what would enhance as well as what obstacles they believed would keep the initiative from being initiated. While some were unique to shipyards, most were typical to what is found in other companies (add on program, insufficient resources to be successful, normal resistance to change, reward system does not recognize efforts on this initiative, etc.).

Activities Required to Enhance Institutionalization

The agents (QA &PI) of this initiative must be able to mentor/coach the targets (and sponsors, if necessary) by suggesting means of "walking the talk" in the journey to institutionalizing CoPQ/Lean-Six Sigma.

<u>Pre-Institutionalization</u>

Several things must be completed, or near completion prior to the communication effort for institutionalizing CoPQ.

1. The first and most important activity for the sponsors to undertake is to accelerate the development and acceptance of the corporate validation method. Not only will this result in bringing the Financial Group on board, but they will become leading advocates for the standard validation method for determining cost avoidance/savings. <u>Without this no one will believe the benefits are real.</u> It is the Principal Investigators belief that NGSS defines validation as being sanctioned by the Finance Group and has the capability of impacting actual corporate budgets. All other forms of defining the benefits of CoPQ and Lean/Six-sigma are *valuation* methods but not *validation* methods and can not be used to adjust budgets, hence the importance of the validation method.

2. Make CoPQ part of the personal appraisal system (PAS). This should be done at each level and should be integrated directly to each person (group) work load. If necessary, reduce work loads (even if it is temporary – this shows the importance of CoPQ) by eliminating non-value added tasks to allow time for CoPQ activities.

3. QA & PI needs to formally link CoPQ to Lean-Six Sigma and then link these activites to ISO-9001:2000 certification and other quality programs. All quality programs should be linked together (this could include any remaining Kaizan activities and perhaps Supply Chain Management activities). Quality reduces variation, which in turn reduces costs and improve customer satisfaction. NGSS needs to explain how all efforts to improve quality and customer focus are aligned to achieve common goals.

4. Finalize the "theme" of the CoPQ institutionalization program and integrate it into all communications. The theme is essentially a means of consistently communicating the same, succinct message about the value of CoPQ to the corporation. An example of a possible theme for this project is:

   The CoPQ system greatly improves the selection of Lean/Six-sigma projects and, consequently, accelerates the ability of the corporation to meet and exceed cost avoidance and cost savings goals.

A corollary to that theme is that:

it provides a means for both executives and workers alike to quantify the enormous opportunity for cost reduction thorough productivity improvement means.

5. Conduct executive awareness training. Executives have many things on their plates, however, they need to have presentations on the importance of CoPQ and Lean/Six-sigma. Once it is confirmed that the executives are on board, suggestions will be made as to how acceptance of the initiative can be enhanced by their actions.

6. Develop a reward system that recognizes those who develop means of reducing costs and creates a culture to sustain those achievements. If NGSS wants to change the culture to a quality, customer-focused culture, these rewards must be meaningful (walking the talk).

Role of Agents in the Institutionalization Phase

The QA & PI group (agents) will have the responsibility of developing the plan to insure that the sponsors are on board and will walk the talk and that the targets are willing adopters of the CoPQ/Lean-Six Sigma approach to quality. Below are some methods to include in the plan for improving communications with each group.

Message to Sponsor (Awareness Training)

All participating departments should begin their meetings with a discussion of quality. This sends a clear signal (walking the talk) that quality (in this specific case, CoPQ and Lean/Six-sigma) are important to the organization. Typical topics for discussion may include:
1. Reports on the potential for cost reduction based on CoPQ reports
2. Reports on successful Lean/Six-sigma projects that have been successful.
3. Questions on how many employees have been trained as Black or Green Belts AND of that group how many have projects? How many have completed their projects?
4. Questions as to whether or not the CoPQ and Lean/Six-sigma projects will be helpful in ISO 9001:2000 recertification? If so, how? If not, why not?
5. Questions on when all cost avoidance/savings projects will be completed? How they might be accelerated?
6. Has Black/Green Belt training been helpful in developing better supervisors/managers?

Typical opportunities for presenting the talk may include:

1. CEO Meetings
2. AOP Meetings
3. Department (VP) Meetings
4. Special Events (Recognition Ceremonies, Lean Events, Six Sigma Training, etc.)

Message to Targets (Successful Adoption Techniques)

The agents (QA &PI) must ensure that the targets (adopters) frequently hear the message of the sponsors (the talk). However their message must also address the "what's in it for me?" question since much of the work of new initiatives that ultimately are designed to help the corporate falls on the backs of the front line workers. This is essentially and equity question. The front line is willing to help but they want new initiatives to be aligned with their current work load or their current work load is modified to make room for the new activities.

The best way to ensure that this happens is to make participation in CoPQ and Lean/Six-sigma part of their PAS goals. However these goals must be integrated into their expected work outcomes and not just be add-ons. Hence, the agents (QA & PI) must work with the front line superintendents and supervisors to determine how best this can be accomplished. Typical messages may include:

1. CoPQ and Lean/Six-sigma are good for you (part of your work)
2. Because it is part of PAS, you will be rewarded for support of CoPQ and LeanSix-sigma
3. Through the Value Bank concept, you and your group have the potential for bonuses
4. Higher quality output from you and your group will enhance job satisfaction (pride in work) which is an important factor in sustaining the gains of the new program
5. Opportunity to understand how your work fits into the corporate goals (cost reduction, ISO 9000, etc.) which also highlights the importance of your work and enhances job satisfaction

Typical Opportunities for Presenting the Talk include:

1. Lean Events
2. Superintendent Meetings
3. Supervisor Meetings
4. Foreman Meetings
5. Six Sigma Training
6. PAS reviews

They will also be available to mentor/coach the agents in delivering the message to the target group. In addition, they will conduct random interviews during the implementation (January –November 05) to get feedback on the effectiveness of the message and whether or not CoPQ and Six-sigma are becoming part of the way NGSS does business and, when necessary, suggest improvements in the implementation plan.

Role of Management in the Institutionalization Phase

While management must "walk the talk" throughout each phase of the change cycle, it is especially important in the institutionalization phase. Also during this phase it is important that good behavior (behavior that reinforces the new culture) is rewarded. and bad behavior (behavior that supports the old status quo) not be tolerated. Management can do this by themselves displaying the new good behavior and by keeping the initiative in place of prominence during every opportunity, such as the meetings previously mentioned. Good behavior can be rewarded through the previously mentioned personal appraisal system and through impact awards. NGSS was committed to doing these things.

Results of Use of Change Management Concepts

NGSS found that the application of the change management model and techniques for the initiate, implement, and institutionalize phases were helpful in introducing and institutionalizing the CoPQ system. Early reports had indicated a sufficient level of acceptance of the use of CoPQ and many of the suggestions of the institutionalization phase were in the process of being put in place. Hurricane Katrina changed all of that. Despite that catastrophe, there is clear evidence that the model developed by the PIs which is based on the worksheets of the three phases of change: initiate, implement, and institutionalize, can assist organizations with successful change At the time of this writing the institutionalization phase was not yet complete, however, early reports indicate a good acceptance of the use of CoPQ and many of the suggestions of the institutionalization phase were put in place such as including CoPQ goals in the individual appraisal systems. In addition some of the elements of the institutionalization phase were begun. This awareness training on CoPQ was conducted with the first group on August 18, 2005. NGSS was in the process of selecting the next group for awareness training as well as the possible scheduling of a meeting with the executives to discuss some of the other items listed under pre-institutionalization (linking to appraisal systems, approval of a "theme", etc). Unfortunately, the greatest natural disaster to strike the United States, Hurricane Katrina, stuck on August 28, 2005.

Hurricane Katrina: It is necessary to make a comment about Hurricane Katrina. Hurricane Katrina was the worst natural disaster to hit the United States in its history. The destruction and disruption of normal life covered a large part of the Gulf South, including the two major shipyards of NGSS (Pascagoula and Avondale). Because of the enormous damage to housing, many workers left the Gulf South and have not returned. In addition, both shipyards sustained severe facilities damage, with Pascagoula receiving the most damage. There also has been a major reorganization among some of the NGSS units involved in this project. The PIs' university, UNO, also suffered major damage and is going through a major reorganization due to projected reductions in the student population. These events caused the project be terminated before the final tasks could be completed. Because of the expected time to recover and the loss of many personnel associated with this project, it is unlikely that the project will be continued. It is possible, NGSS will use some of these lessons learned to restart a similar program.

FEMA Proposal Example

The last example we will cover deals with a consortium of three companies from Louisiana submitting a proposal to the Federal Emergency Management Agency (FEMA). The three companies were KETA LLC, a Native American tribally owned company, THE RESOURCE FOUNDATION, INC, a 501 (c)(3) non-profit company, and Prescient, LLC, a New Orleans based small business. The proposal was a unique concept for changing the way FEMA approached disaster readiness relative to Command and Control, including public interaction using a series of call centers linked via a state-of-the-art Information Technology (IT) architecture.

The president of the lead company, Prescient, had been exposed to change management concepts as outlined in this handbook. Since this proposal expected to change the way a major government agency operated, the President of Prescient decided to apply the change management techniques to the proposal. This was done primarily through the use of the initiate, implement, and institutionalize worksheets. The President of Prescient provided background information on the use of the worksheets and went over them in some detail and then asked key senior managers associated with the proposal from each company to complete the worksheets. The completed worksheets were then used as the basis of a discussion as to how well the proposal included the important change management factors (selection of sponsor, agent, target, etc.)[4].

The results were not only interesting, but valuable in the improvement of the worksheets themselves. When the President of Prescient reviewed the results he found the worksheets to be effective but believed that the responders had not done as good a job as he expected. Since these were seasoned managers he wondered why. The conclusion he came to was that they needed a true change management mentor to help them through the questions. When he informed me of this I immediately thought of organizations real need for in-house change management competency personnel. This further lead me to think of the concept of Six Sigma in which a large number of company employees are trained in the details of this quality approach and are attached to each company Six Sigma project to mentor them in the process. Most of this training of these in-house experts consists of the development of large numbers of Six Sigma Green Belts and Black Belts. For those unfamiliar with this terminology refer to the many excellent books and articles on Six Sigma[1]. The concept of Six Sigma is also discussed briefly in Chapter 10, Six Sigma and Change Management. We will discuss change management competency in more detail later, but let's first consider some of the important observations the President of Prescient made. These observations resulted in improvements in the worksheets and how they considered the written response. Those changes were made and are incorporated in the worksheets that appear in this handbook.

When using change management techniques, it is often not possible to anticipate all of the misunderstandings and subtleties that will come up when applying these techniques. This fact, by itself, supports the idea that there is a need for an internal expert in change management to assist company employees in correctly applying the concepts, but let's see if we can make some simple changes in the worksheets that will minimize these misunderstandings. One of the first things noted in the review was that when a consultant, rather than an internal employee, pushes the proposal there is an opportunity for misapplying the concepts behind the roles people play. Consultants and companies outside of the funding organization often make these types of proposals in response to a Request for Proposal (RFP). Such was the case in this FEMA example. In this case, because the consortium initiated the proposal, some of the responders considered themselves the sponsors. However, when dealing with change management, sponsor has a specific definition, that is, the sponsor is the one who can legitimize the change. This means he/she has the resources (budget or funding) to make the change happen. Thus only persons in the organization with the funding (the one asking for requests for proposals) can fill this role. In fact, all of the roles of persons involved in change management (sponsor, agent, target) must come from the funding organization. However there are some subtleties which can occur and must be explained. For example, once the sponsor awards the contract, the consultant could easily fill the role of agent even though they would require a single contact point in the organization funding the initiative. Hence, the change agent team could consist of both consultants and in-house persons.

Another subtlety or duality can occur when the sponsor in the funding organization is not convinced of the value of the proposal. In this case, in the initiating phase, the sponsor must also be treated as a target, that is, someone who has to change. This is true even though a "target" within the organization has been designated in the proposal because unless the sponsor can be persuaded to change his/her opinion about the proposal then the proposal never gets out of the initiate phase and there is no need to worry about who is the "ultimate target". Again, this was the case in the FEMA proposal. Government agencies are difficult to change and to suggest that FEMA change the way they approached disaster recovery represented a major change for FEMA and hence a major hurdle for the proposing consortium. Getting the consortium to understand that the FEMA authority sponsoring the RFP must also be treated as a target in the initiate phase was very helpful to the team. So one of the important lessons learned in this application was that, despite the strong interdependency of the three phases, there could exist conditions in which the roles could change in each of the phases. Hence, the explanations which accompany the worksheets were modified to clarify these subtleties. However, as stated earlier, the best solution still appears to be the availability of an in-house change management expert to clarify these issues as they occur[5].

One might ask, are there organizations that have internal change management groups that give the organization a change management competency which allows them to smoothly apply these techniques to company initiatives? The answer is yes and I had the occasion to work briefly with one such organization. This was Northrop Grumman Information Technology located in Virginia. They have a Technology Change Management Group and I gave a joint presentation with the leader of that group in 2003[6,7]. Much more will be said about that when change management competency is discussed in more detail in Chapter 10.

Your Own Company Examples

These examples were designed to give you some confidence that others have applied these methods and they work. However, what each of you need to do is to develop some benchmarks of your own, otherwise, you will not have the confidence to apply these worksheets on future projects. So get busy with some examples, use both projects that failed and those that were successful.

Suggested Exercises

1. Take past examples of changes your company implemented, compare the method used then with the methods (worksheets) suggested here. Would the projects have been improved if the worksheets had been available, explain?

2. Take a new project and develop the worksheets for the initiate and implement phases. Involve the project team in these steps. Which steps were the most useful to the team and why?

Notes

1. Lannes, W. J. and Cheramie, W.J., Louisiana Power & Light Company, Priest, W. and Whilhelm, M.R., Seimens-Allis, *230 KV Operation of Substation Designed for 115 KV by Controlling Voltage Transients,* IEEE Transactions on Power Delivery and Systems, Spetember, 1984.

2. Scott, P.W., Page, P.E, and Windam, T.M. Woodside Offshore Petroleum Pty Ltd.,
Applying Technical Limit Methodology for Step Change in Understanding and Performance, 1996 IADE/SPE Drilling Conference, March, 1996.

3. Scott, P.W. and Bond, D.F., Woodside Offshore Petroleum Pty Ltd. *Setting and Achieveing Technical Limit Goals in Well Construction by Enabling the Talents, Energies and Attributes of People,* 1998 Offshore Technology Conference, May, 1998.

4. Savoie, Robert, *Engineering Management 6097 Report on Utilization of Change Management Worksheets, Summer, 2006.*

5. Private conversations between the author and Bobby Savoie concerning the significance of the report on the utilization of the change management worksheets.

6. Lannes, W. and Guenterberg, S. *Managing Technology Change,* presentation in New Orleans, March, 2002.

7. Lannes, W. and Guenterberg, S.*Technology Change Management,* presentation at the
Stennis Space Center, Mississippi, January, 2003.

Chapter 10

SIX SIGMA AND CHANGE MANAGEMENT

When you cannot express it in numbers, your knowledge is a meager and unsatisfactory kind.
Lord Kelvin

Certainly Lord Kelvin would have liked Six Sigma because it is all about numbers. My close associate, Dr. Baha Inozu, a Six Sigma practitioner, loved to save, "In God we trust, everyone else bring data!" While I doubt if that statement was original with him, he constantly repeated it to emphasize that Six Sigma is data driven. For those of you are familiar with Quality Programs you will recognize that Six Sigma is one of the more significant approaches to improvement to come out of the Quality area.

Six Sigma was developed in the United States by Motorola in 1987 and has been adopted by many major companies, most notable, General Electric.[1] Many companies have Six Sigma programs today. Most have explored them because of the concrete financial benefits that have been demonstrated by such companies as General Electric.

Six Sigma has many peculiarities, including its name, and I shall briefly address some of them for the benefit of the reader before I make the connection between Six Sigma and Change Management. The concept of Six Sigma is related to the normal distribution and its spread, or variation, which is generally expressed as sigma. For example, a normal distribution with a variation of three sigma means that the probability is 99.73% that its samples will fall within the three sigma region. In quality programs the number of samples are usually designated as opportunities. So said another way, if there were one million opportunities in the sample space of a three sigma normal distribution then only 2,700 opportunities would be outside of the three sigma range. Those outside the range are called defects or defects per million opportunities (DPMO). A defect is any variation of a required characteristic of the product or its parts, which is far enough removed from its target value to prevent the product from fulfilling the physical and functional requirements of the customer or internal quality standards. For a four sigma normal distribution there are only 64 DPMOs. So as you might guess, for a six sigma normal distribution there are not going to be many DPMOs, in fact there is less than one (0.002, which is actually two defects per billion opportunities)!

However, most readers are familiar with the proposition that the goal of Six Sigma is to reduce the variation to only 3.4 defects per million opportunities. That is true, and is one of the peculiarities of Six Sigma. When Motorola introduced this method, they included a 1.5 sigma shift to address the fact that in dealing with real world problems it was not possible to be this precise (a true Six Sigma). They believed this adjustment would provide a more realistic outcome for processes repeated over many cycles. With this shift, the Six Sigma variation is the commonly quoted 3.4 defects per million opportunitites. For a more detailed discussion of the 1.5 sigma shift see any good book on Six Sigma.[2]

Another peculiarity of Six Sigma is the use of Karate terms such as Green Belt, Black Belt, and Master Black Belt. This are terms which designate how much training the person has in applying quality improvement and statistical techniques to process improvement projects. The quality improvement techniques range from simply brain storming techniques to more elaborate approaches such as design of experiments. It is in the recording of outcomes of many repetitions of the observed process that gives Six Sigma its data driven reputation.

The six sigma approach aims to reduce defect levels to only a few parts per million for an organization's key products and processes. While this requires the effective use of statistical principles and various tools for diagnosing problems and facilitating improvement, it can be simply thought of as having the goal of "doing it right the first time". To accomplish this high level of achievement, Six Sigma uses what is know as DMAIC, which is explained below:

DEFINE
- Identify the work you do (your Product/Service)
- What do you need to do your work (your Suppliers)
- Identify who your work is for (your Customer)
- What are the 'key characteristics' of your product/service?
  (i.e. 'Critical To Quality': those features/requirements that most
  directly affect your Customer's satisfaction with your product/service.)

MEASURE
- Map the process.
- Evaluate the measurement system.
- Measure the current performance of the process.

ANALYZE
- Analyze the capability of critical measurements in the process.
- Analyze variation in key characteristics and determine what controls the variation.

IMPROVE
- Reduce variation and/or eliminate defects in the process.
- Eliminate non-value-added steps/processes

CONTROL
- Implement control plans to monitor/maintain improvements over time.
- Continue to reduce variation and eliminate defects, toward Six Sigma performance

The reason I have provided this much detail on the Six Sigma methodology is not to try to make you experts in Six Sigma but, as you shall see, this methodology ties nicely into change management principles. Along those lines, there is one other Six Sigma practice which I need to introduce, that is the Six Sigma Project Charter. The success of each Six Sigma project is very dependent on a good Project Charter. The Project Charter has a very specific format and uses Six Sigma names such as project Champion. A sample project charter is shown below:

Project Information		
Project Name:		Entry Date:
Project Start Date:	Completion Date:	Submitter:

Project Team			
Champion:			Process Owner:
Team Leader:		Staff Support:	Student Support:
Change Management Lead:			
Strategic Plan Lead:			
Proj. Selection/Publicity Lead:			
Lead Green Belt Candidate:		Green Belt Candidate:	
Master Black Belt/Mentor:			
Project Type:			
Black Belt Green Belt			

Project Details	
Project Description:	
Business Case (Benefit):	
Problem Statement:	
Process Boundaries (Scope): In: Out:	
Start Event	Stop Event:

Project Improvement Criteria			
Metric Type:	Baseline:	Current:	Goal:
Metric Type:	Baseline:	Current:	Goal:

Project Improvement Criteria			
Metric Type:	Baseline:	Current:	Goal:
Metric Type:	Baseline:	Current:	Goal:

Comments:

Project Milestones				
			Tollgate Review (Signature required for approval)	
	Phase	Completion Date	Champion	Process Ownder
	Project Charter			
D	Define		Signature	Signature
M	Measure			
A	Analyze		Signature	Signature
I	Improve			
			Signature	Signature
C	Control			
	Final Briefing		Signature	Signature

If you will take a close look at the Project Charter it includes many of the change management principles we have been presenting in this book. Note they even recognize the need for a Change Management Lead on the team. What is not shown on this example (which we used for our University of New Orleans process improvements projects) is a Financial Lead. Many people are now doing that; it is particularly important to have someone with a direct link to the Accounting and Financial Group, particularly when you are trying to actual capture the benefits. If you recall earlier it was stated that capturing the benefits was one of the more difficult things to do. If the person on the Project Charter Team, that is linked to the Accounting and Financial Group, is actually a member of that group that is even better. Ideally, the Accounting and Financial Group could assign a person as the Financial Lead on several Project Charter Teams. This will greatly enhance the potential for actually capturing the benefits. In companies like General Electric, who saved billions of dollars through their Six Sigma program, it is obvious the Six Sigma Program had strong ties to their Accounting and Financial Department.

Note in the Project Charter form they also ask what is the business case for this project? They also require that specific measures be developed to determine the success or failure of the project. Note too that there are two important persons named on each project. They are the champion and the process owner. The champion assumes the role of the sponsor as defined in the earlier chapters and the process owner is the target.

In large companies (and often in small companies also) it is often difficult to identify the process owner. I believe this is why lasting process changes are difficult to sustain. In the case of the University of New Orleans we had lengthy discussions about who was the process owner on the three processes we were trying to improve. Eventually in each case someone finally said , " I guess I am the process owner". This represented a very big step in not only solving the problem but in maintaining the solution once it was implemented.

In many large companies the process under consideration will often involve elements of many departments such as engineering, manufacturing, and purchasing. Generally each of these departments has their own budgets and personnel and usually manage both to meet departmental goals; this means that when multi-departmental tasks or processes are involved the solutions are generally sub-optimal. This is because persons controlling these multi-departmental processes are usually thought of as 'coordinators' without any real authority. Hence, most are reluctant to claim the title of process owner. This is due, in part, to the fact that the company reward system is usually not set up to recognize this type of work. However having to identify the process owner on the charter is essential to the success of the project. The champion (sponsor) should be involved in this discussion and should be in a higher enough position to get the departments involved to accept the authority of the process manager; in other words, he must be senior enough to legitimize the assignment of the process owner. Recall from our past discussion of the determination of the sponsor we may have to move up several layers in the organization to make sure he has authority over all key participants in the project. The selection of the champion should follow the same rules for the selection of the sponsor.

In recent years, companies have been combining process improvement programs such as Lean and Six Sigma.[3] Lean was developed by Toyota and is a method for locating and eliminating all non-value added tasks in the process. An example of combining Lean and Six Sigma might be a cycle time reduction project. Lean tools might be applied to stream-line an order entry process. This examination of the process to eliminate non-value added tasks could lead to the discovery of significant rework (incorrect addresses, etc). Six Sigma tools might then be used to drill down to the root cause of the problems and identify the solution. However in most cases these combined approaches have retained the use of the Project Charter concept developed in the Six Sigma approach. Let's then take a look at a comparison between Six Sigma and Change Management. First let's look at a comparison between the initiate, implement, and institutionalize phase of change with the Six Sigma methodology, DMAIC.

Change Management Steps	Lean Six Sigma Steps
Iniate	Develop Project Charter Define Phase of Six Sigma
Implement	Execute charter process Measure, Analyze, Improve and Control Phases of Six Sigma
Institutionalize	Permanently change process by implementing recommendations

It is easy to see that following the DMAIC process recommended by Six Sigma takes you through the three phases of change management. Note that it is built around the Project Charter process. Let's now take a look at the relationship between sponsor, agent, and target and the roles defined in the Project Charter process.

Change Management Roles	Lean Six Sigma Roles
Sponsor	Champion
Agent	Team Leader/Black Belt/Green Belt
Target	Process Owner

Again we see a strong correlation between the roles of change management and the roles required on the Project Charter. What we are observing is that the Six Sigma approach to process improvement has build into it many of the principles of change management that are required for the successful initiation, implementation, and institutionalization of change initiatives. Note that the milestones and the use a financial link from the team to the organization is one of the prime reasons Six Sigma has been so successful in outstanding financial results (capturing the benefits). Hence, while there is no doubt that the proper use of Six Sigma requires knowledge of statistics and quality improvement tools, much of its success can be attributed to the build in change management processes. Said another way, all new initiatives that are successful must have change management techniques and principles built into them. This supports the concept of the importance of change management skills for organizations; that is, for an organization to be successful they must have a high degree of change management competency. What we have observed is that Six Sigma has processes which give the organization a built-in change management competency.

Change Management Competency: This was first mentioned in Chapter 9 in the FEMA Proposal Example. Let's return to that discussion. As you may recall it was suggested that in order to successfully deploy change management techniques that organizations needed a cadre of change management experts whose sole responsibility is to insure that the organization is successful in introducing change. Clearly this group must keep up to date on change management and be available to whole organization. How can this be done? Let's go back to the Technology Change Management Group in NGIT mentioned in Chapter 9.

Northrop Grumman Information Technology established the Technology Change Management group several years ago to provide a competitive advantage. The group still functions today in NGIT. The purpose of the group was similar to what was suggested by the President of Prescient, that is, to improve the success rate of IT projects as measured by the standard on-time, on- budget parameters. In regard to on- budget, the change management team had to reduce the cost of the project through the application of their change management techniques. The change management team had to continually convince the new initiative teams of their actual worth to the bottom line. In this way they were similar to the Six Sigma teams[3].

They believe in-house change management competency was superior and more cost effective than outside consultants. Their strengths were that they knew the culture of the organization and the political traps to avoid, they knew the people involved in the change and hence what would resonate well with them so that their help could be enlisted, and because of the manner in which the group was formed they were well respected in the organization. They keep up with current change management changes through formal training, weekly team training and specialized change mentoring.

Formal Training: NGIT provided two internal courses on technology change management training. One course was for anyone who wanted to attend (understanding and awareness along with increasing sponsorship for the initiatives were the goals of this course) and the other was a three day course for those who would implement a change on a project or within the organization. They also conducted weekly team training for those in the Technology Change Management group. These meetings were on all NGIT projects that were implementing changes and were an excellent opportunity for mentoring and updating change management skills on actual projects. These team meetings also included team topics.

At NGIT the more experienced team members would often mentor others who were first embarking on a change after they had received the formal training. This specialized change management mentoring would often happen for at least one to two hours per week to bring the project through its first change cycle. In addition to this specialized change management training, the head of the group conducted training for the more experienced members. For those projects that were implementing Capability Maturity Modeling (CMM) and Capability Maturity Modeling Integration (CMMI) there was extensive training on the model and examples of how projects had implemented those requirements. Hence, there was a great deal of training to implement and sustain a change management competency in NGIT[4].

Change management competency in organizations is a real competitive advantage. The NGIT example shows how one company implemented and sustained this core capability. It is clear that there needs to be a plan to develop this type of competency and it must include a lot of training, both formal and informal. Note in the NGIT case, they continued to sharpen their skills on actual projects. As a minimum change management competency should have training on three levels, 1) awareness and background training, 2) intermediate level training for beginning practitioners, and 3) advance training for those involved in mentoring the teams and project leaders. At levels 2 and 3, the training must include application training on actual projects. Generally this type of training involving three levels and application projects will initially require outside assistance from change management consultants.

Suggested Exercises:

1. Discuss the importance of internal change management competency to sustaining changes (institutionalization).

2. Compare the Six Sigma Project Charter Approach to the Change Management Worksheets. Which provide the most value? Can one be used on smaller projects or should they both apply to all projects. Note that the worksheets provide insight into some of the questions asked on the Six Sigman Project Charter approach (i.e., what is the business case).

3.Use the Six Sigma Project Charter approach to past projects (both successful and failures). What did you learn from this exercise?

References
1 Evans, J. and Lindsay W., The Management and Control of Quality, Sixth Edition, Thompson- Southwestern, 2005.
2.Pande, P, Newuan, R, and Cavanagh, R., The Six Sigma Way: How GE, Motoraola, and Other Top Companies are Honing Their Performance, 2000.
3. Private correspondence between the author and Sharon Guenterberg, 2006.

Chapter 11

INTRODUCING CHANGE INTO ORGANIZATIONS IN CRISIS

It's the last straw that breaks the camel's back.
Anonymous

We have already made the case that change is difficult even when you have a thorough understanding of the principles of change and its impact on individuals and organizations. This becomes all the more difficult when the change initiative is introduced into organizations which are already experiencing stress. In the old saying shown above, the last straw implies that it is a small thing, but when it is added to the already overstressed person or organization, it becomes the trigger for the exploding or imploding of the organization or breakdown of the individual.

In the fast paced, highly competitive world today, overstressed organizations are more the norm than the exception. That being the case, we had better have an approach to introducing change under these conditions. Fortunately, we do. It not only includes the concepts we have introduced earlier in initiating, implementing, and institutionalizing change, but it includes concepts relating to coping under stress. Coping under stress relates to Conner's concepts on an individual's ability to assimilate change[1]. This is the primary theme of Conner's book, Managing at the Speed of Change . He states that change initiatives are generally successful when introduced at a speed in which the organization is capable of assimilating.

Hence, when introducing change into organizations in crisis, one important consideration is the assessment of the ability of people and organizations to assimilate change. Individuals are affected by three levels of assimilation, micro, macro, and organizational. They are defined as:

micro – those changes that come from family and friends
macro – those changes that come from larger organizations or associations such as professions, church, or race
organizational – those changes introduced in the workplace.[2]

Understanding in which place your people and organization are in regard to their ability to assimilate new change will help you in deciding how to introduce the change with minimum interruption. In most cases, individuals are affected by all levels to varying degrees meaning that they are under considerable stress. This which means the organization should try to minimize stress wherever and whenever possible. In earlier days, management took the position that personal problems should be left at the door when you reported for work. Considering how micro events can significantly affect a person's performance at work, this was not a very enlightened approach. Fortunately in recent years, lead often by quality initiatives, management has come to the conclusion that happy employees mean happy customers and much more attention has been paid to understanding and addressing employee concerns. Many of the most successful companies are listed on annual list of _Fortune's 100 Best Companies to Work For._ Many include such services as on site day care as well as many other amenities not usually seen in past years.

As a manager you need to understand the types of events which are most stressful for your employees. Over the years, healthcare personnel and others have developed lists of events which put stress on individuals. They usually begin with such events as loss of a spouse down to experiencing a minor traffic violation. The primary point is that when employees have several of these stressors acting on them, particularly if they are events at the high end of the list, they may not be able to handle new initiatives. If the individuals in the group are in this condition, then the new change initiative, even if relatively small becomes the straw that breaks the camel's back. To mitigate this, management needs to employ a tactic known as pacing.

Kathleen Eisenhardt and Shona Brown in their book, Competing on the Edge, make use of this concept of pacing[3]. The book is all about companies that are in competing on the edge of chaos, in the area of bounded instability described in Chapter 3. These companies are in area in which they can be the most creative and competitive and in which change is most likely to occur. The authors make the point that even in companies that are used to change, it takes a lot of energy to maintain that position of bounded instability and even they must occasionally slow down to remain successful. This is known as pacing and essentially relates to Conner's concept of moving at the speed at which the organization can assimilate the change.

As an example, coaches who know the capabilities and strengths of their players build their strategies around those capabilities. What makes the team even better is when the coach realizes that he needs to change the momentum of the game in order to let his team adjust. Despite the fact he may have great players, they sometimes get out of synch and play in a dysfunctional manner. What is needed is a timeout and to let them catch their breath (mentally). This is an example of pacing and often they return to the game and play the style of play of which they are capable. Management needs to be able to do the same thing. Understanding how much your organization can assimilate and when to apply pacing is particularly important when introducing change into organizations in crisis.

The point has to be made that there are two distinct categories of introducing change into organizations in crisis. The first is when the change is the result of the crisis, the second is when the organization is in crisis but the new change initiative does not have any direct connection to the reason the organization is in crisis. We will discuss the difference shortly but let me talk first about the first category, when the change is the result of the crisis. Unfortunately, here at the University of New Orleans, we had a perfect example; Hurricane Katrina. Hurricane Katrina struck the Gulf Coast of the United States on August 29, 2005 resulting in the largest natural disaster to strike in the history of the United States. All the changes that were occurring to the citizens of New Orleans and the students of the University of New Orleans were a direct result of Katrina. At the time of this writing we were approximately eight months after the event and still many New Orleanians were still living with neighbors and relatives, or in trailers, or waiting for trailers. Many jobs had been lost, many had to change schools, in other words, almost everything we had in our old comfort zone had been disrupted or no longer existed. So as an experiment I distributed one of the stressor lists (loss of spouse to minor violation) to the students in my change management class of about thirty students. The list had 39 items of which 27 were micro stressors and the rest macro and organizational. I then asked them to check off each item that applied to them since August 29, 2005. I then put categories of 0-3, 3-5, 5-10, 10-15, and greater than 15 on the board and surveyed the class. While we had some in every category, the majority fell into the 5-10 stressors category, which is quite a lot of stress. I then asked the class, if you were a manager and this class was your workforce what would you know about your workforce? All agreed that they would probably have a tough time assimilating any new change. I then followed up with a question about preparation for a hurricane so I need to tell you a little about that. When the hurricane season approaches, residents on the coast are advised to prepare a hurricane kit consisting of a battery powered radio, bottled water, and other survival items. In that package you are advised to take all important papers such as insurance, birth certificates, etc. I then asked the class, are you ready to get your important papers together in case of another storm? The responses were not unexpected. Despite what looked like a simple task (particularly to a person outside a hurricane prone area) it became the straw that broke the camel's back. Most literally groaned, several said if they had to do that again in the upcoming hurricane season they would pack up and never come back. Most were dismayed at just the thought of having to do that and actually exhibited the same signs of combat fatigue which comes from repeated high stress, often of the same type.

Now in the story above, the person asking the questions (myself) had also gone through Katrina and the post Katrina problems (some of which are described above) so I was aware that they would be literally stunned by the thought of preparing for a similar event again, as would I. The point is, however, that in many organizations management is often not well connected with the needs and concerns of employees and if they try to introduce new initiatives when the workforce is severely stressed (as are the Katrina victims) it will surely fail. Hence it is extremely important that, as managers, we are fully informed of the capabilities of our employees to assimilate change. While this takes a great deal of a manager's time it is certainly not wasted time for as we will see in the last chapter, employees are truly our most important asset and they deserve all the care and protection we are capable of providing.

On small teams it is often possible for the team leader or work supervisor to get to know the ability of his/her employees to assimilate change. But how do you do it in larger organizations? Fortunately, as in the case of assessing the current culture of organizations, there are companies who specializing in assessing the capability of organizations to change, the potential for resistance to change, and related topics[4]. There is another method worth mentioning here, but it can be time and energy intensive, and that is the ADKAR approach as advocated by the editors of the Change Management Learning Center in their book, <u>Change Management: the people side of change</u> and on their website www.change-management.com[5].

In the ADKAR case you evaluate each individual to be affected by the change, normally by interview, some sample questions are shown below. The ADKAR model is an effective tool for individual change management. The ADKAR model presents five stages that individuals go through when making a change, ADKAR is an acronym for the following categories:

1. **A**wareness of the need to change. Communicating the reasons to change is necessary. Asking questions like "Do you understand and agree with the business reasons for making this change?" would help find the awareness level

2. **D**esire to participate and support the change. Addressing their inherent desire to change to improve their participation. Asking questions like "Do you want this change to happen or would you prefer to keep things the way they are? What would cause you to want this change to happen?" would help with improving desire.

3. **K**nowledge about how to change. Can be improved with education and training needed for the skills and behaviors that are required by the change. Asking "Do you know about the change and the required skills to support the change?" would find areas of training on which to focus.

4. **A**bility to implement new skills and behaviors. Ability can be improved by developing new skills and behaviors with ongoing coaching and support. Asking questions like "Are you capable of performing these new skills?" would gauge the employee's ability.

5. **R**einforcement to keep the change in place. By addressing the necessary elements that are present to keep the person from reverting back to old behaviors we can effectively reinforce the change. Asking "Are you receiving the necessary support and reinforcement to sustain this change?" would find new rewards and recognition programs.

The resulting information is useful in developing training and other preparatory exercises to prepare the individuals for change. For example, if desire is the only category with a low rating, management can drill down further to determine the reason; i.e. is it because the individual sees no value to him/her in the initiative, is it because they have no ability to assimilate another change, etc.? While this is useful, the interview process can definitely put the individual on the spot and they may be reluctant to give honest answers, particular if the organization has a history of removing persons who do not get on board with the new initiative. So this process could add even more stress. On the other hand, surveys as discussed above are anonymous and often you will get a better read on the capability of the individual to assimilate additional change[4]. In any case, you need to develop a means of determining the assimilation capabilities of individuals and organizations so that you can develop a pacing plan to introduce the change in a manner in which it will have a higher chance of success.

While skill in applying pacing can help in the successful implementation of change initiatives, another approach can often avoid the need for pacing. That is, the willingness of management to reduce existing workload, this may preclude or delay pacing. This is true even if the reduction of workload is temporary to make room in busy schedules to accommodate the new initiative. While this makes sense, particularly if an organization is already overloaded and overstressed, it is seldom considered as an option. For an overstressed organization this is really an essential step.

So how do you reduce workload since your boss says everything is important? That is an important question which can only be answered by a true prioritization process. This should include as a first step an analysis of the tasks the organization must do. One simple, yet effective approach is to do a Quality Grid[7]. While working in the utility industry we hired a company, ODI, to assist us in developing our quality program. They introduced us to an assessment tool for improving both our productivity and quality of our processes, it was the Quality Grid. The Quality Grid was aimed at evaluating the day to day tasks of an organization for alignment and execution. The alignment portion was aimed at answering the question "Is this what my customer expects?" which, said another way, is am I doing the right thing – is it a value added task? Execution was aimed at answering the question "Am I doing the work the right way?" which, said another way, is this the most efficient and effective way of getting this done? The idea was to identify the most important tasks and time consuming tasks (usually no more than 20) being done on a repetitive schedule and place them in one of four categories; (1) right things done right, (2) right things done wrong, (3) wrong things done right, and (4) wrong things done wrong as shown in the Quality Grid in Figure 10.1

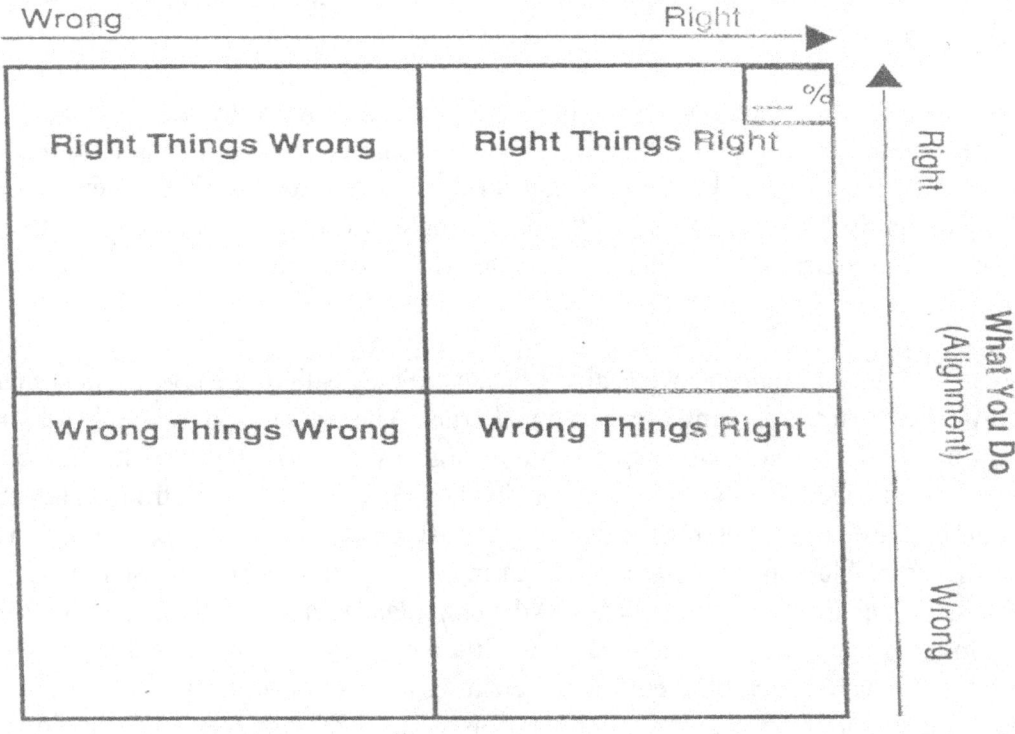

Figure 10.1: The Quality Grid

For our discussion the important point here has to do with wrong things which can be described as non-value tasks. Non-value tasks can become institutionalized in organizations many ways, one is a process that was important when initiated but is never eliminated even though it is no longer relevant. The important point here is that all non-value added tasks should be eliminated. This could be the first area in which you look to unload workload; this has a double benefit it that it provides additional time for the new initiative while also eliminating work that was not helpful to the organization. However, it can also be a non-value task that is required by law or regulation in which case it can only be eliminated by changing the regulation or law. An example of this is the regulation that all companies which have lists of customers must provide detailed privacy information informing the customers that they do not give this information to other parties.

These notices are typically never read by customers since most consider it junk mail. However it takes a great deal of money and time to comply with this regulation. Fortunately in this case, banks, retail stores, and others affected by this non-value requirement have been having some success in lobbying the regulators to relax or eliminate this requirement. This is not the normal outcome, most of the time you must live with this problem and although it takes time and energy you can not eliminate it. Those "wrong" things that are not driven by regulations or law can usually be changed, even though it may be a major culture change. Many efficiency consultants who are hired to improve productivity call this step of eliminating non-value added tasks, "work destruction". There are usually more opportunities to eliminate work than is generally realized.

But what do you do if, in fact, you do not have any non-value added tasks to eliminate (they could all be required by law or regulation)? Then you must defer some of the required work for a period of time to give the organization an opportunity to absorb the new initiative without becoming dysfunctional. Then if this unloading of work is still not sufficient to allow the organization to assimilate the change at a rate which it can handle, then pacing will be required.

Let us go back to the difference between changes that are the result of the crisis versus changes that are different from the existing organizational crisis. The primary difference is that in the first case, it is not necessary to develop a sense of urgency because the crisis itself, which is the cause of the change, is going to be very obvious (such as Hurricane Katrina). The unique thing about this case is that you must treat it as you would a medical triage case or like a case of a very serious problem in a plant or manufacturing facility. In these cases you must (1) stop the bleeding, (2) stabilize the situation, and (3) develop plans to mitigate the crisis[6]. This is not necessary in the second case in which the new initiative is not directly related to the present crisis in the organization; the problem here is creating a sense of urgency. This is important since the change is not related to the crisis it is common for the organization's employees to ask, "Why do we need to do this now, can't you see we already have too much to do?" Shown below is a chart showing the differences in the approaches, notice that while there are many similarities there are, indeed, some differences. The primary difference is that in the first case, some management and leaders may need to be changed and in the second case a major problem may be in convincing the organization of the urgency of doing the new initiative now.

1. If Crisis is the Reason for the Change	2. If Crisis is not the Reason for the Change
Get buy-in on need for change and create a sense of urgency. Since major crisis exists this should be easy but must be communicated in a concise and consistent manner (reasons for change).	Must create a sense of urgency and develop buy-in why the new change is necessary now (since organization is already overloaded).
If current crisis was due to poor leadership and management, change leadership or bring in a strong consultant with broad powers from the Board. Must be aware of the assimilation capability of organization/individuals	Must be aware of the assimilation capability of organization and individuals. That is, develop a sense of *prioritization and urgency* because an organization which is already overloaded will ask why do we have to do this now?
Quickly address the crisis by 1) *stop the bleeding, 2) stabilize the situation, and 3) develop plan to address cause of crisis.* This is similar how a doctor would address a problem in the Emergency Room or how a plant engineer would address a serious plant problem.	Unload workload, even if it temporary (will show importance of change being done *now* and indicates understanding of situation, i.e. already stressed group)

Increase communications in all three phases of the initiative (initiate, implement, instutionalize). Develop implementation plan into steps. Unload workload, even if it temporary (will show importance of change and indicates understanding of situation, i.e. already stressed group Be prepared to modify as conditions dictate (pacing). Make sure each step is fully implemented and institutionalized before going to next step.	Increase communications in all three phases (initiate, implement, institutionalize). Develop implementation plan into steps. Be prepared to modify as conditions dictate (pacing). Make sure each step is fully implemented and institutionalized before going to next step. Continue to monitor emotions of people and be prepared to adjust schedule (pacing)
Manage the Past Emphasize what was right with old organization and what will not change (retain core values, etc.) **Manage the Present** Tell them what will change. Communicate that old solutions no longer work and implement a new plan to move on (new solutions). Get buy-in on why the new solution is the best and achieveable. Develop a sense of urgency to adopt the change. **Manage the Future** Once organization is stabilized develop vision for new organization. Reward the new desired behavior and punish old behaviors. Begin living and doing the new vision.	**Manage the Past** Emphasize what was right with old organization and what will not change (retain core values, etc.) **Manage the Present** Tell them what will change. Communicate that old solutions no longer work and implement a new plan to move on (new solutions). Get buy-in on why the new solution is the best and achieveable. Develop a sense of urgency to adopt the change. **Manage the Future** Once organization is stabilized develop vision for new organization. Reward the new desired behavior and punish old behaviors. Begin living and doing the new vision.

Table 10.1.

Katrina has given us many examples that fall into the Case 1 type of situation. For example, as a result of Katrina many residents of the Gulf Coast and New Orleans did not return to their homes. Some opted to take jobs in the cities to which they evacuated while others were delayed in their return due to the need to keep their children in a stable school environment for a full school year or because they could not get closure on their insurance claims in order to restore their houses. The total result of this was businesses and schools which were dependent on the pre- Katrina levels of population quickly got into trouble. This was true at the University of New Orleans, and other universities in New Orleans, which are heavily dependent on the tuition from enrollments for operating revenues. Tulane University, an old established private university, was the first to announce staff and faculty reductions. Loyola, Xavier, and Dillard, all private institutions followed in restructuring plans. The last to announce the restructuring plan was the University of New Orleans (UNO). UNO used the methods described in Table 1 in an effort to provide stability for its students and faculty.

UNO College of Engineering Use of the Change Crisis Methods: Hurricane Katrina struck the Gulf Coast of the United States on August 29, 2005 creating the largest natural disaster to ever hit the United States in its history. The University of New Orleans, located, on the shores of Lake Pontchartrain in New Orleans, not only suffered damage to its campus, about one third of the campus was under water, but with the displacement of the residents of metropolitan New Orleans it lost its student body and faculty. Despite this disaster, the University of New Orleans (UNO) was able to offer courses via the internet and off site locations for the Fall 2005 semester (the Katrina Semester). UNO was the only university in the City of New Orleans to offer any classes that semester. Other major universities such as Tulane, Loyola, Dillard, Xavier, and Southern University of New Orleans offered no classes that semester. UNO was able to service approximately 7000 of its students through internet courses that semester. The student body was approximately 17,500 at the beginning of that semester (pre-Hurricane enrollment).

The devastation to New Orleans and the Gulf Coast was overwhelming. Hundreds of thousands had to evacuate and could not come home because their homes were not in any condition to be reoccupied. This brought about the next crisis for the universities (actually all schools) which attempted to open the following Spring 2006 semester in January 2006. Most residents had not returned and the student body population was not sufficient to support faculty and staff at pre-Katrina levels. Many schools, at all levels, were required to lay off faculty and staff to keep their operating budgets in balance. At the university level, Tulane University was the first to announcement cuts in faculty and programs. These cuts included eliminating most of the engineering programs and Newcomb College, the women's program at Tulane. Obviously this was met with dismay from alumni and faculty/staff. These announcements were shortly followed by similar announcements at Dillard University, Xavier University, and Loyola University, all, like Tulane, are private institutions.

The University of New Orleans was one of the last to announce their restructuring plan. This was due, in part, because they are a publicly supported and are part of the Louisiana State University (LSU) system. To legally create a restructuring plan UNO had to get the LSU System to declare a state of Financial Exigency, the equivalent of bankruptcy. This was finally done in late April, 2006. Once they received approval, UNO also eliminated programs, departments, colleges, and tenured faculty. This restructuring caused a major crisis on campus for students, faculty, and staff.

The Dean of the College of Engineering (COE) at UNO was provided with the methodology for introducing change into organizations already in crisis. This situation matched the conditions of introducing a change which was the result of the crisis. While the crisis was caused when the hurricane devastated vast regions of the city (at the height of the catastrophe eighty percent of the City of New Orleans was underwater), the real problem was the destruction of housing which precluded residents and students to return to the city to resume their lives. UNO gets only about 25 percent of its operating budget from the State of Louisiana by being part of the LSU system. The remaining funds to operate the university must come primarily from student tuition. Hence with the projected loss of thousands of students, the faculty and support staff would have to be reduced. It is the law in Louisiana that State Universities must submit balanced budgets, hence restructuring was a necessity.

The Dean decided to approach the problem utilizing the steps recommended in the methodology for introducing change into organizations in crisis. These steps are: (1) stop the bleeding, (2) stabilize the situation, and (3) develop a plan to address the cause of the crisis. Within that structure, he would develop an approach to managing the past, present, and future. In managing the future he developed a vision of what the College of Engineering would look like in two years. This vision was extremely important to a demoralized college and university, in particular, it was important to retain the good faculty and staff which would become part of the recovery team.

Stopping the bleeding: Clearly UNO had to bring its budget into balance. This was done through a UNO restructuring plan which included the College of Engineering. The criteria for the removal of programs, departments, and colleges were primarily based on the value of the programs to the mission of UNO as an urban university. It also included other factors such as the historical record of student enrollments, programs with consistently low enrollments would become candidates for elimination. Obviously this was a painful process for everyone concerned, however the restructuring plan did stop the bleeding. For COE, it resulted in the elimination of the Department of Engineering Management (more about that later), one Associate Dean position, and two additional tenured faculty positions from other departments, the loss of two open positions in one department, and the loss of all Teaching Assistants. All colleges and administrative units had to go through a similar process to balance the budget.

Stabilize the situation: This is the step in which managing the past, the present, and the future become important. Managing the present means to remove as much anxiety as possible from the present bad situation. Managing the past means that since this crisis was due to circumstances created outside of UNO and the College of Engineering, that the Dean needed to make sure that everyone knew that much of what was done in the past was good and should be continued. It is important for organizations to know what will be continued and what will not be continued. Managing the future is also important to reducing anxiety since if the future looks bright down the road, many will stay focused on that goal and be willing to sacrifice in the short run.

Managing the Past: The College of Engineering at UNO was known for its ability to produce very capable engineers for industry. While this ability was not well known outside the region, within the region local industries sought after the graduates of the COE programs. This is due, in part, to the fact that most senior faculty remain committed to classroom teaching even when they maintain a strong research program. The Dean reminded the faculty that would not change due to this crisis. When things are in a massive state of change, it is important that everyone know what will change and what will not change, particularly when it is a *core value such as teaching excellence.* In conjunction with the excellence in teaching was another strength which is a corollary to teaching. That is, COE has a strong commitment to its students and stays in close contact with them through a *strong advising system.* In addition to the solid teaching reputation and strong advising system, COE has a School of Naval Architect and Marine Engineering (NAME) which is one of only three in the United States and which enjoys a world wide reputation. Since we are located in one of the premier shipbuilding areas (the U.S. coast of the Gulf of Mexico) we receive excellent industry and government support. *NAME has the largest undergraduate enrollment in the United States and will remain the lead school in COE.* In addition to these strong core values which will be maintained during and after restructuring, the past performances and can do spirit of the COE faculty must be remembered and given full recognition and thanks. During the "Katrina" semester they were asked to convert many of their courses to internet format within a period of about twenty days. Many of the faculty had never taught in the internet format, yet COE put together a comprehensive set of courses which allowed students to continue their pursuit of a college degree. As mentioned earlier, UNO was the only university to offer courses to their students in the New Orleans area, and COE played a major role. With little time to catch their breath, faculty was once again called upon to offer more than their normal course load in the Spring 2006 semester to further encourage students to return to the classroom. Once again the faculty, despite the fact that many of them had lost their homes and were displaced themselves, responded. The Dean wanted them to know that this extraordinary effort had not gone unnoticed and thanked them for this exceptional effort and asked them to hang on and carry over this can do spirit into the recovery period following the completion of the restructuring plan.

Managing the Present: The primary purpose of managing the present is to reduce anxiety which will help to stabilize the situation. One of the first tasks to be done is to complete all activities pertaining to the restructuring plan and to get that activity completed as soon as possible. Unless this was done quickly, it would be difficult to focus on the task of moving forward. To accomplish this, the Dean made contact with all of those directly affected by the change and while an unpleasant task, made every effort to make the change as smooth as possible. This is important because the remaining members were watching to see how those members who had been eliminated were treated. In many cases their elimination may not have anything to do with their individual performances and the remaining members, who often think - that except for a little luck that could have been them, want to see that they are treated with respect and dignity. Fortunately in this case the two tenured professors were senior enough to retire and there was a clear willingness to assist other displaced members to find employment. In the case of the eliminated program, the graduate program in Engineering Management (ENMG), the program was able to be saved even though the department was eliminated. This was made possible because it was a graduate only program as well as being interdisciplinary. The College of Business (COB), which was the interdisciplinary partner with the College of Engineering in the ENMG program, was already running several graduate only MBA types of programs without having a department for each. It was jointly agreed that the program could continue under the COB umbrella with COB providing the administrative support and COE providing support through adjuncts and offices for adjuncts and graduate assistants. Hence, to the student the move was transparent to them since the curriculum, courses, and degree did not change. By these actions the Dean made it clear that despite the needed reduction, he cared about the faculty and students who were affected most.

Once the restructuring tasks were completed in a timely manner attention had to be focused on the remaining faculty and staff whose energy and expertise would be required to provide the momentum for the return to normalcy and beyond. The Dean encouraged all Department heads to talk individually with each faculty member to insure that their concerns, needs, and wants were addressed and that they were aware, that despite the short term difficulties, the vision for the College of Engineering was very positive. In conjunction with that, to insure that the future was positive the Dean worked with the Chancellor to make certain that all damaged laboratory equipment was repaired or replaced in a timely fashion, particularly since re-accreditation would occur in 2007 and preparations must begin this Fall 2006. The building repairs were also needed to be accelerated so that it would be fully functionally by Fall 2006. The Dean also encouraged Departments and Student Organizations to help in the sprucing up of the building in such areas as the Tau Beta Pi garden area as well as providing uniform name information on all rooms. Lastly the Dean recognized that an organization which is already under stress can easily become dysfunctional if the work load is not monitored. Hence he indicated that the most important short term goal was to prepare for the accreditation visit so he delayed or modified some of the usual requirements such as the annual Strategic Planning meeting.

The Strategic Planning meeting usually takes a full day and is taken seriously since the plan is monitored during the year to make sure it is not simply put on the shelf. It does take a lot of preparation and time, however, so the Dean decided to concentrate only on the short term goal of preparation for the accreditation visit and allocated that strategic planning day primarily to presenting his plan to recover from the crisis and for those departments that wished to, to use the remaining part of the day for collecting and reviewing class folders which are required for accreditation. He also encouraged his Department Chairman to look for opportunities to unload work or delay it while the college is going through this transition period. He further indicated that he was aware of the continuing stress on the college and would continue to monitor the progress of the college and, if necessary, would institute "pacing". He explained that pacing is something used by innovative companies which introduce many changes. It recognizes that companies function best when the pace of change is at a rate that the employees can assimilate. They recognize that it is better to occasionally slow down rather than cause dysfunctional behavior because the changes are overwhelming the work force. It is an approach that allows the employees to catch their breath in order to forge ahead.

Managing the Future: As mentioned above the group which remained after the restructuring were seriously worried about their futures. One major factor in retention of the remaining workforce was the vision of how COE would look two years down the road. The Dean felt that two years was long enough to get a good feel on how the city, region, and university would look from an infrastructure and a student population point of view and yet not too far out so that remaining faculty would see improvements as too far away. The first positive outcome for UNO engineering of the Katrina storm was the removal of the basic engineering programs from Tulane University. This left UNO as the only university in New Orleans offering engineering degrees. UNO offers Bachelors, Masters, and PhD degrees in engineering. Because of the role of engineering in rebuilding the area and its strong link to the urban mission, the Chancellor reiterated his commitment to the College of Engineering as one of the lead colleges in the recovery of UNO. This means that when financial conditions improved there was the real expectation that COE would be provided higher than normal funding to achieve its goals of excellence in engineering education. In addition, the departure of Tulane from the engineering field had resulted in a vastly increased interest by local firms in supporting UNO engineering with funding. In addition, the Chancellor promised to have all of the laboratory equipment destroyed by the storm replaced within plenty of time for the Fall Semester of 2007 accreditation visit. The Dean also noted that the numerous research centers associated with the college were already showing signs of recovery and it was expected that the centers would be in very strong positions in two years, particularly those supported by DARPA and NASA. Hence it is very plausible that UNO engineering will be in a much stronger position in two years than they were even prior to Katrina.

Develop a Plan to Address the Cause of the Crisis: The crisis which required the restructuring was the expected loss of thousands of students. Hence a plan to increase the number of students should be developed now so that in two years the enrollment is approaching or exceeding pre-Katrina levels. This will be done in conjunction with the overall UNO plan for recruitment but already there are some things in place to help the College of Engineering. First the replacement of damaged laboratory equipment. This means that by the beginning of the Fall Semester many of the labs will be brand new with state of the art equipment. This will certainly appeal to prospective students. Second is the newly availability of scholarships earmarked especially for engineering. This means we can approach members of the top ten percent of targeted schools and let them know they could qualify for a full four year scholarship. These scholarships can be for undergraduate or graduate. The potential for more funding from our support organizations for brochures, mailers, and radio spots to point out the advantages of an UNO engineering degree appears to be almost certain. To accomplish an improved recruiting program the Dean will appoint a recruitment committee and others that would be recommended by the faculty to develop plans to mitigate the crisis by October 2006 ready for full implementation for Fall 2007. The committee will consist of faculty and members of the COE Industry Advisory Council.

This approach was reduced to a set of PowerPoint slides and presented to the full faculty on May 18, 2006. The Dean began the meeting with a 25 minute video on building a house in less than three hours.[8] This was done to set the tone that with good plans and teamwork it was possible to overcome huge obstacles and accomplish major feats. The result of this meeting, which was the last faculty meeting before the summer break, was a re-energizing of the UNO College of Engineering with an understanding of the need for the restructuring and the realization that we could not only come back from this disaster but it appeared very likely we would be in an even stronger position within two years. The Dean credited the methodology for introducing change to organizations in crisis with this positive outcome.

While handling change when the existing crisis is a result of change is extremely important because if improperly handling the results can be catastrophic, the second case of introducing change into an organization in crisis when the change is not related to the crisis is more common. If improperly handled, this too can lead to very bad consequences.

Not understanding how much your organization and its key people are already stressed when you introduce change is unfortunately very common. Hence, in every change initiative some sort of assessment of the ability to assimilate another change should be done. With proper training of key managers and supervisors (and with senior management support) this can often be done by the organization, however, there are numerous consulting firms which can assist in this assessment. This was mentioned earlier when the assessment of company culture was discussed. Once you know your organization and its employees' ability to assimilate change you can develop a plan to initiate, implement, and institutionalize change. It may require examining existing priorities and workloads and could involve pacing, but properly planned many organizations have shown the ability to successful manage change in organizations that are highly stressed.

Introducing change into organizations in crisis happens much more frequently than you might expect. In fact, it is probably safe to say that most of the time when a new initiative is initiated, the organization is already under a great deal of stress. Hence understanding how much additional work the organization can assimilate is extremely important. Using the approaches outlined in this chapter will be very helpful. These approaches are based primarily on two significant articles relating to initiating new initiatives in organizations in crisis; they are: (1) Change Through Persuasion by David Garvin and Michael Roberto and (2) Driving Organizational Change in the Midst of Crisis by John Carrol and Sachi Hatakenaka.[9,10] These are two actual cases, the first involves changes required at teaching hospitals and the second involves changes at a nuclear plant. It is recommended that you read these articles; these two case studies will provide additional evidence of the effectiveness of the methods discussed in this chapter.

Suggested Exercises

1. Discuss the pros and cons of using the ADKAR approach with each individual versus using an anonymous survey.

2. Discuss why it is difficult for many organizations to eliminate non-value added work. Offer some solutions.

3. Use the Quality Grid as an exercise for analyzing the distribution of right and wrong things in your work group.

4. Read the Harvard Business Review article, *Change Through Persuasion,* then list examples from this case study of (a) managing the past, (b) managing the present, and (c) managing the future.

5. In the UNO case in this chapter, what was the most important thing the Dean did? Why?

Notes

1. Conner, Daryl, *Managing at the Speed of Change*, Villard Books, 1993, page 74.

2. Conner, Daryl, *Managing at the Speed of Change*, Villard Books, 1993, page 79.

3. Brown, S. and K. Eisenhart, *Competing on the Edge: Strategy as Structured Chaos*, Harvard Business Press, 1998, pp. 161-188.

4. Conner Partners, which was previously ODI, specializes in change management and beyond and has numerous instruments and articles for determining the readiness of organizations to change, see www.connerpartners.com. The principal in Conner Partners is Daryl Conner.

5. *Change Management: the people side of change* and their website www.change-management.com

6. Carroll, John and Hatakenaka, Sachi, *Driving Organizational Change in the Midst of Crisis,* IEEE Engineering Management Review, Third Quarter 2001, page 18.

7. ODI, a Quality Consultant firm in the 1990s presented this Quality Grid in their custom developed material for Entergy Corporation while I was still working for Entergy. I have used this as a simple, yet effective self-assessment tool both in industry and in academia.

8. The Two Hour House

9. Carroll, John and Hatakenaka, Sachi, *Driving Organizational Change in the Midst of Crisis,* IEEE Engineering Management Review, Third Quarter 2001

10. Garvin, David and Roberto, Michael, *Change Through Persuasion,* Harvard Business Review, February, 2005.

Chapter 12

THE REAL CHANGE AGENTS

"He who seizes the right moment, is the right man."
Goethe

Up to this point we have been advocating methods and principles that can be applied with much success to ensure that change actually happens. We have already seen that there are specific roles that people must play in change, these are the roles of sponsor, agent, target, and advocate. Hence, in every case, someone has to eventually apply the methods and principles. That "someone" will be the men and women in every organization who must put the principles into practice. Like a good team in sports, good coaching and game plans are essential. But without good players in the skilled positions, the team will not be competitive. Hence, the success of any change depends, in large part, on the people who play the roles of sponsor, agent, target, and advocate.

The importance of people is exemplified in a quote from a veteran plant manager in a 1998 article first published in the *California Management Review*. He said:

> We've talked a good game for decades, but it has only been in the last few years of my career that we have translated the belief that people are critical to our success into a management philosophy and practice that leverages the full potential of our people.... Technologies must be there to succeed, but without a motivated, educated, and committed work force, long-term success will be a struggle.[1]

Companies that understand and practice this will have a real competitive advantage. However, while many companies say that their people are their most important assets, not all companies "walk the talk" when it comes to their people. In fact, in a recent article, Peter Drucker states, " Employers no longer chant the old mantra 'People are our greatest asset'. Instead, they claim 'People are our greatest liability'." [2] The point he makes in the article is that outsourcing is becoming a major industry because, if a worker is outsourced, then the enormous time required to comply with the numerous employment laws and regulations will be handled by the firm providing the outsourced person. This includes any lawsuits which may result due to problems associated with contract persons. Clearly, the firms who want to get out of handling laws and regulations associated with employees see their employees as liabilities rather than assets. How does your company view its people? Does your company spend the appropriate resources on recruiting and retaining people, particularly key employees? Does your company maintain its training and workforce during business downturns, or are they the first to be reduced? How much value does your company place on its employees?

My experience in the Marine Corps taught me the value of the individual Marine in accomplishing the mission assigned. Because of the importance of the individual Marine, Marines spend a great deal of time in training. Marine boot camp is world famous for its effectiveness and is aimed at providing needed skills and proper attitude for the individual Marines. Advanced training follows boot camp and is aimed at building teamwork. The smallest Marine infantry unit is actually called a "fire team." They also train in special small unit skills such as "immediate action drills" so they will react by instinct when "surprised" by ambushes and other difficult situations. Perhaps of more importance is that they are trained in the traditions of Marines. They are taught to understand the importance of the Marine motto, "Semper Fidelis," always faithful. Respect for individuals and teamwork have made Marines famous for their effectiveness, particularly in fast changing environments such as the battlefield. Even their recruiting efforts emphasize the importance of the individual Marine. An example of this is their long running advertisements saying they need "A Few Good Men." The success of the United States Marine Corps serves as a good example of the need to value your people.

Before you say, " But we are not Marines and we can't do that.", I would like to share with you a true story about a private organization which had a long history (actually over a century) and was part of a culture that generally hired people for life. They were very traditional and were not open to change but their plant manager decided he needed major changes of both the disruptive (radical) and incremental (continuous) type. He achieved all of his objectives without firing old employees or hiring new ones. He did it by changing the employees he had. By concentrating on respecting and improving his existing employees, he achieved remarkable results. This story is told in an article in the Sloan Management Review. The article was written by Robin Copper and M. Lynne Markus and was titled, "Human Reengineering." [3]

I use "Human Reengineering" during a segment of a course I teach. The segment is a study of the reengineering revolution began by Hammer and Champy with their book, *Reengineering the Corporation.* . While reengineering had quite a few notable successes, it also had many failures. In fact, both Hammer and Champy wrote follow-on books in an attempt to address the short comings.[4,5] What was perhaps worse, reengineering had become closely associated with downsizing. "Human Reengineering" directly addressed that issue in describing an example in which the company was able halve the size of a crew on a production line while not laying off any employees. The manager was Toshio Okuno and the plant was one of the three top soy sauce plants in Japan. He also achieved some other rather remarkable results by employing several other innovative techniques. His techniques are certainly worth further study but I would like to return to the major point of this article, that is, when deploying new processes, you have to first address the capabilities of the people who will be introducing the changes. A paragraph from the beginning of the "Human Reengineering" article is worth repeating.

Increasingly, it is becoming clear that the engine of reengineering is not reengineering analysts, but managers and the people who do the work. Reengineering requires committed, empowered people, not simply to operate processes *after* they have been reengineered, but also to reengineer them in the first place.

No matter which reengineering consultants your company might employ, one step in the methodology always remains the same: design teams are staffed by people who perform key activities in the process that is being redesigned. So the success of reengineering hinges critically on these people and their knowledge, creativity, and openness to radical change.

This, coupled with a paragraph near the end of the article, succinctly emphasizes the importance of people to the process. The concluding paragraph states:

> The first and most important lesson is that lasting organizational change always requires significant change in people. Without change in human knowledge, skill, and behavior on the job, change in technology, processes, and structures is unlikely to yield long-term benefits. It is essential to focus on changing people as well as other aspects of the organization, because people make the difference in organizational performance and have ideas for productive change.

Changing people in a significant way is what the Marines also realize. This is what makes them successful. When the recruit comes into the system, he is radically different from the type of person the Marines need. This is one of the primary purposes of boot camp and the advance training, to change the individual so that he will have the skills and behavior that make him a United States Marine. With these new skills and attitude, the new Marine is ready to join the Marine team and to meet the challenges in a manner expected of Marines. This can also be done in industry and that is what Mr. Okuno achieved. He changed the skill set and attitudes of his employees to make them more productive. You can also do this in your company. Employees want to do well. You can help them by training and example to become the types of people who will make your change initiatives successful.

How important are people? Well Silicon Valley is well known for its entrepreneurial and innovative companies. Many believe that it is the people that make Silicon Valley what it is. Some say the mystery of the Valley is related to the almost religious-like culture. To sustain that success, it must continue to attract people with that same type of attributes. Listen to what one of the premier executive search consultants says about the type of people they seek in Silicon Valley:

> They must either already share the faith and embrace the religion, or see it and 'convert'. Though the faithful here cannot imagine anyone hesitating to join them, recruiting to local companies has never been an easy task. Many from outside Silicon Valley have only worked in traditional corporate cultures with political bureaucracies and, when told of the realities of working in the area, are skeptical. But experiencing is believing, and after working in Silicon Valley many become converts, and like many converts, more zealous in their faith. <u>Without the faithful and the converts, Silicon Valley's growth</u>

<u>would slow and the culture would be irrevocably altered.</u> [7] (emphasis by author)

What the search consultant is essentially saying is that without sustaining and recruiting the right people, even Silicon Valley will cease to be competitive. People do count, they are your competitive advantage!

We have touched on recruiting (Silicon Valley) and developing talent from within (the Soy Sauce Company). It should be noted that successful companies do both well. To return to the Marines for a minute, it is worthy of note that in the late 1970's the Marine Corps decided to placed the responsibilities for recruiting and basic training under one commanding officer, thus breaking the long-held tradition of separating the two functions. In order to be successful they felt that both were essential and part of the same concept of producing productive Marines.[8] I personally think one of the best development programs are programs that empower people. In a previous chapter we indicated that many managers and supervisors did not understand empowerment. When done properly, empowerment not only makes organizations more productive but these programs also build future leaders. Always remember that developing leadership and people to their highest potential is the work of line managers and supervisors, not the Human Resources Department. It is your job, they can help but never forget it is your responsibility. In a recent article in Harvard Business Review the authors of *Growing Talent as if your Business Depended on it,* state, "Many executives believe that leadership development is a job for the HR department. This may be the single biggest misconception they can have."[9]

While this book has presented principles and templates to help you be successful in initiating, implementing, and institutionalizing change, it is really the people who make the difference. People are not only your most important asset; they are your only <u>unique</u> competitive advantage. Treasure them, support them, award them, and they will help to change the world for you.

Suggested Exercises

1. How does your company approach training? Does it support personal development skills?

2. How does your company approach recruiting? What types of questions do they ask applicants? (If possible view Stanford University's Executive Briefings Video, *Implementing Strategy: Managing Through Organizational Culture* - it makes some interesting points on questions asked during recruiting).

3. Does your company have an empowerment program? How does it work? Is it empowerment only in content or does it include context (see discussion on degrees of empowerment in Chapter 3).

4. Does your company "walk the talk" when it comes to people? Justify your answer with examples.

5. If you were the CEO, how would you recruit and develop people? How does this compare with your current procedures?

Notes

1. Longenecker, Clinton, Timothy Stansfield, and Deborah Dwyer, "The Human Side of Manufacturing Improvement". IEEE Engineering Management Review, Summer 1999, pages 93-103.

2. Drucker, Peter; "They're Not Employees, They're People", Harvard Business Review, February 2002, pages 70-77.

3. Cooper, Robin and M. Lynne Markus, "Human Reengineering", MIT Sloan Management Review, Summer, 1995.

4. Hammer, Michael and James Champy, "Reengineering the Organization" HarperBusiness, 1993.

5. Champy, James, "Reegineering Management", HarperBusiness, 1995.

6. Hammer, Michael, " The Reengineering Revolution", HarperBusiness, 1995.

7. Lee, Chong-Moon, Miller, William, Hancock, Marguerite, and Rowen, Henry, *The Silicon Valley Edge: A Habitat for Innovation and Entrepreneurship,* Stanford University Press, 2000. pages 346-347.

8. Carrison, Dan and Walsh, Rod, *Business Leadership -The Marine Corps Way,* MJF Books, 1999, page 24.

9. Cohn, Jeffrey, Rakesh Khurana, and Laura Reeves, *Growing Talent as if your Business Depended on it,* Harvard Business Review, October 2005, page 66.

Epilogue

*"It is not the strongest of the species that survive, nor the most intelligent,
but the one most responsive to change."*
Charles Darwin

Our journey along the path of the change cycle has come to an end. While it is not the evolutionary journey referred to by Darwin, it is a long journey none-the-less. This book was intended to be a helpful companion on the trip. Many have taken the journey before you and have successfully institutionalized change. You can, too. This book should help you to now see change as normal, something that is always happening, like the growth of your children. And like the growth of your children, it may be a journey that you actually enjoy.

Now you have tools and principles to assist you in the initiating, implementing, and institutionalizing change. Remember to always answer the basic questions associated with change such as: (1) Who is the sponsor for the change? (2) Who is affected by the change and how? and (3) How are the benefits of the change measured and captured? By doing so, you will greatly increase your chances of success.

In addition to these three basic questions, you also have other tools, such as the project relationship organizational chart and the worksheets associated with each phase of the change cycle. These will assist you in going through the change cycle journey. Perhaps the most important thing to remember is the impact that culture has on change initiatives. Culture will impact all change, but it is particularly important when initiating major change. The primary criteria for a major change is that it is very different from the way things are presently being done. Major change has nothing to do with complexity or cost. Rather, it has to do with whether or not the change is aligned with the current culture.

Understanding your existing culture often takes the help of an outside consultant. If your assessment indicates that your existing culture and the proposed initiative are very much out of alignment, you must change the culture before you initiate the change. Most agree that changing the culture in incremental steps enhances the chance of making the change last. If the change is lasting, they you have successfully institutionalized the change.

About the Author

William "Will" J. Lannes, III is no stranger to change. He has had three careers in three different industries and is directly connected to a fourth through his role as Director of a major Savings Bank, a position he has held for over 25 years. In each of these careers he has been involved in major change. Upon graduating from Tulane University with a Bachelors of Science in Electrical Engineering he entered the United States Marine Corps where he stayed eleven years in various assignments between two very different specialties, infantry and electronics. While in the Marine Corps he received his Master of Science in Electronics Engineering at the U.S. Navy Postgraduate School in Monterey, California. His military career included a tour in combat in Vietnam as the operations officer of a Combined Action Group, the USMC unique pacification program. He was awarded the Bronze Star for his leadership abilities in Vietnam.

After leaving the military he joined Louisiana Power & Light Company where he held various assignments in both system design and operations, and in production. He led several large engineering groups in both areas at the Vice President and Senior Vice President level. While involved in system design, he designed and energized the first uprated substation in the United States. This design pushed the envelope in high voltage design. While involved in production, he helped to initiate the first "partnering" program in the power plants. During the later part of his career, the electric industry went through major changes in regard to deregulation and in his last assignment he helped the parent company, Entergy, form a new strategic business unit to provide direction for the entire Entergy system transmission and generation capabilities. After twenty-two years in the electric industry he took early retirement and entered the world of academia full time.

Will joined the University of New Orleans in 1992 as the Associate Dean of Research and Graduate Affairs in the College of Engineering. He led an interdisciplinary team which developed and implemented a new graduate program in engineering management. The program was authorized in 1996 and he has served as the founding Director of the Engineering Management Program in the College of Engineering. When the program achieved departmental status, he became the first Chairman of the Engineering Management program. In 2006 he retired from this position but was awarded Professor Emeritus status and continues to be affiliated with the University of New Orleans.

His efforts have not gone without recognition. For his pioneering work in high voltage substation design he was elected a Fellow in the Institute of Electrical and Electronic Engineers (IEEE). He was also selected as the IEEE Outstanding Engineer for Region 3, a six state area. He has published numerous papers and has been an invited speaker at professional meetings and conferences. He was presented the Prize Paper Award by the IEEE Power Engineering

Society. He was elected to Who's Who in American, Who's Who in Engineering and Science, Who's Who's in Industry and Finance, Who's Who Among America's Teachers. He remains active in his profession and is a registered professional engineer in the State of Louisiana.

This book is an outgrowth of his experiences and his teaching of courses in engineering management, in particular his course on managing technology change and his course on change management. His university research as also directly contributed to the worksheets which he has developed for initiating, implementing, and institutionalizing change. His current specialties are change management, total quality, productivity improvement, and technology transfer. Professor Lannes remains active teaching seminars and consulting on change management subjects.